THE JUDAICA IMPRINT
FOR THOUGHTFUL PEOPLE

The Story of Rebbetzin

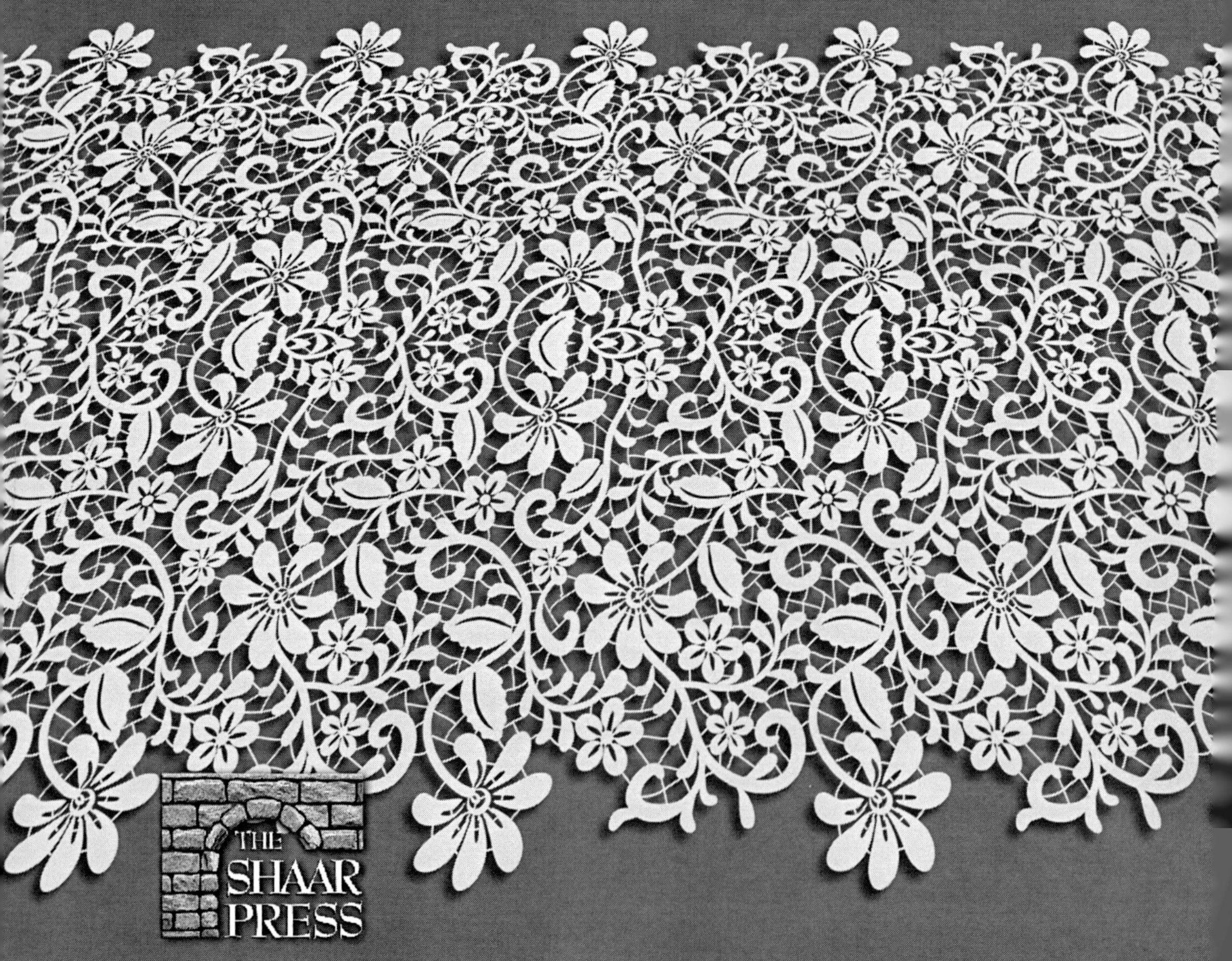

A BIOGRAPHY FOR YOUNG READERS

Henny Machlis

HER AMAZING HOME AND FAMILY

Rabbi Nachman and Miriam Zakon

FIRST EDITION
First Impression ... May 2018

Distributed in Europe by
LEHMANNS
Unit E, Viking Business Park
Rolling Mill Road
Jarow, Tyne & Wear, NE32 3DP
England

Distributed in Australia and New Zealand
by **GOLDS WORLDS OF JUDAICA**
3-13 William Street
Balaclava, Melbourne 3183
Victoria, Australia

Distributed in Israel by
SIFRIATI / A. GITLER — BOOKS
POB 2351
Bnei Brak 51122

Distributed in South Africa by
KOLLEL BOOKSHOP
Northfield Centre, 17 Northfield Avenue
Glenhazel 2192, Johannesburg, South Africa

THE ARTSCROLL YOUTH SERIES®
THE STORY OF REBBETZIN HENNY MACHLIS

4401 Second Avenue / Brooklyn, N.Y. 11232 / (718) 921-9000 / www.artscroll.com

---

ISBN 10: 1-4226-2069-7 / ISBN 13: 978-1-4226-2069-4

Typography by CompuScribe at ArtScroll Studios, Ltd.

Printed in the United States of America
Bound by Sefercraft, Quality Bookbinders, Ltd., Brooklyn N.Y. 11232

דברים היוצאים מן הלב נכנסים אל הלב

This book brings us great joy — documenting the צדקות of our beloved Rebbetzin, Henny Machlis, ז״ל, and inspiring others to also use their abilities to uplift the world. Her תורת חסד showed us the beauty of, and inspired us to live, a תורה-observant life. Our life is so full of ברכה because of what we learned from her and her family. We will forever be indebted for the extraordinary impact she's had on who we are.

We dedicate this invaluable work in memory of
our honored grandparents, ז״ל:

פייגא בת אסתר מרים ושלמה ❖ נחמן דוד בן פרל ואברהם הכהן
אסתר לאה בת פרל רבקה והרב אלעזר הרץ ❖ שמואל בן שיינא בריינא ובן־ציון הכהן
חיה דבורה בת שרה ריבה וחיים ❖ דב בער בן אסתר ואהרן
חנה בת אסתר וצדוק

And in honor of our revered grandfather, יבדל לחיים טובים וארוכים:
דוד בן ביסל ושמואל
who have been the role models of תורה and מידות that serve as
the foundation for the entire family for generations.

We further dedicate this monumental work in honor of our cherished parents, שליט״א:

אמי מורתי פרל רבקה בת אסתר לאה ושמואל הכהן
ואבי מורי מרדכי יוסף בן פייגא ונחמן דוד הכהן
אמי מורתי העניא טובה בת חיה דבורה ודב בער
ואבי מורי בנימין יהודה בן חנה ודוד

Their integrity and unshakeable commitment to core תורה values earn them the respect of all and establish them as pillars of their communities. We are forever grateful to them for everything, and particularly for gifting us a genuine love for our people, raising us around constant hospitality, and placing מידות above all else.

With our heartfelt ברכה to our holy children הי״ו:
אהרן נחמן הלל הדסה מרים נועה תפארת
May each of you continue to be the greatest of children, developing your individual strengths, and especially the מידות of our holy Rebbetzin, Henny Machlis, ז״ל.
May you continue being so caring, sensitive, loving, generous, conscientious, helpful, friendly, happy, positive, creative, curious and thirsty for knowledge and truth in the genuine תורה tradition.
May you be blessed בכל מכל כל and see and appreciate every ברכה.
May each day be greater than the day before.
יברכך ה׳ וישמרך; יאר ה׳ פניו אליך ויחנך; ישא ה׳ פניו אליך וישם לך שלום

We are immeasurably fortunate to have a close personal relationship with our venerated life guide, HaRav Mordechai. We lovingly bless our Rebbe and his beautiful family, שליט״א:
יהי רצון שכל נטיעות שנוטעין ממך יהיו כמותך.

Table of Contents

PHOTO CREDITS:

Jared Berstein Photography
Machlis Family
Betzalel Messinger
Joan Roth
Eugene Weisberg Photography

Thank You!

We could not possibly begin a book about Rebbetzin Henny Machlis *a"h* without saying, "Thank you." As you will see later, Henny felt very strongly that showing gratitude is hugely important. And she was so right!

So here are just some of our thank-you's:

- Our thanks, first and always, to Hashem, Who has given us so very much. All of our abilities, all of our opportunities, and of course all of our blessings come from Him, and we humbly say thank You.
- We also want to say, "Thank you," to someone we never met — Rebbetzin Henny Machlis. As we learned more about her amazing life, we were very inspired. Henny was always a great teacher, and she taught us so much about loving our fellow Jews and loving Hashem.
- A huge thank-you to Rabbi Mordechai Machlis, Moshe Machlis, and the entire Machlis family. They were all so positive, so friendly, so helpful, and so much fun (especially the grandchildren who we spoke with!). Rebbetzin Henny loved them all very, very much. May they continue to give her much *nachas*.
- This book is based on ***Emunah with Love and Chicken Soup***, the biography of Henny Machlis written by Sara Yoheved Rigler. She is both a brilliant writer and a wonderful person, and we thank her for all the major efforts she put into learning about Henny and her life that enabled us to write this book.
- Over the years, the staff at ArtScroll have become like family. They are always there for us, whenever we need something.

The list of our friends there is too long to write here, but you all know who you are — and to all of you, we say, "Thank you for everything."

- And of course, we want to thank our readers — you! We know everyone is busy, and we appreciate that you are taking the time to read this book. We hope you will enjoy it as much as we enjoyed writing it.

Rabbi Nachman and Miriam Zakon

A note about Rebbetzin Henny Machlis

A rebbetzin is someone who teaches and guides Jews in the Torah way, and that's exactly what Rebbetzin Henny Machlis always did. But she was always very informal and humble, and many people called her by her first name, Henny. We've chosen to do that in this book, because we felt she would have wanted us to.

Now turn the page and prepare to read about someone totally amazing!

Prologue

It's Friday night in Yerushalayim. In the neighborhood of Maalot Dafna, in a small apartment, a unique Shabbos meal is taking place. Close to a hundred people are being hosted by the Machlis family.

Peeking in, we can see all kinds of people sitting together enjoying their Shabbos meal. Some of the visitors observe the Torah and the mitzvos, others are not yet religious. There are Sefardim and Ashkenazim, and even some non-Jews. There are girls from seminary and lonely, homeless people. Somehow, everyone manages to fit into a living room that's big enough for maybe fifty people. There is room for all. Everyone has a place. There is food for everyone — good food, and lots of it! — provided and prepared by the legendary Rabbi Mordechai and Rebbetzin Henny Machlis, and their fourteen children! All for free!

People know that if you don't have a place for Shabbos, you can always drop in at the Machlis home for meals. The poor, the lonely, the forlorn find a home and a meal at the Machlises. Other people come, not because they need a place to stay, but because they want to feel the love, warmth and remarkable *hachnassas orchim* atmosphere: to observe in wonder Rebbetzin Henny Machlis, the always-smiling mother of a large family, serving her numerous guests with joy and energy, making each one feel special.

Many, many people's lives were changed through attending Shabbos meals at the Machlises. Many walked away with the feeling that they had seen a modern-day version of Avraham Avinu and Sarah Imeinu. The Machlis hospitality reminded them of Avraham and Sarah, who spread belief in Hashem through their *hachnassas orchim* to the

Rabbi Mordechai and Rebbetzin Henny Machlis

many desert wanderers they fed in their tent. Only this "tent" was a simple apartment in modern-day Yerushalayim.

Sadly, Henny passed away in 2015, so you will never meet her. But in this book you will read about her life. From the incredible and unusual stories related by those whose lives she touched you will learn why she became one of Jerusalem's most beloved personalities. Reading about her may or may not change your life. But it will certainly change the way you do *chesed,* and it will strengthen your *emunah,* your faith and trust in Hashem.

Enjoy reading about how a regular girl from Brooklyn became a Jerusalem legend.

CHAPTER 1

Bringing Shabbos to the Whole World

You would imagine that someone who is keeping an open house and feeding so many guests would make it easier on themselves by serving just the Shabbos-meal basics. You know: ready-made fish loaves, soup, chicken and cholent, and maybe a kugel or salad. That would make it easier and keep the costs down. But Henny Machlis's heart was so big that she bought, prepared and served all the basics — plus three different types of kugels, all kinds of salads and a choice of four (yum! four!) desserts. Vegetarian guests? No problem. Every Shabbos included vegetarian cholent and vegetarian main dishes. And, of course, there were plenty of second helpings for everyone who wanted.

The practice at the Machlis Shabbos table was that everyone at the meal was given the opportunity to introduce themselves and speak or teach. There were, however, two rules. They were: When speaking, no politics were allowed. And nothing could be said that would offend religious Jews. Other than that the conversation was open to all questions and topics, and, of course, *divrei Torah* and Shabbos songs.

The rules

Numbers were meaningless to Henny. One Purim she got a call from Rabbi Jeff Seidel. Jeff devotes his time speaking with people who are not yet religious who come to visit the Kosel. He arranges for them to experience Shabbos and Yom Tov meals at religious homes. Jeff was excited. Thirty

Meaningless numbers

students from Tel Aviv University had just shown up and asked him to arrange for them to see what Purim was like in a religious home. What a *kiruv* opportunity! Many of these students had never been to a real Purim *seudah* ever. Who knew how many of them would be inspired by what they saw and want to find out more about connecting to Torah!

But Jeff had a problem. This group came to him at the last minute, late Purim afternoon. That was when families had begun their meals, their homes overflowing with guests. How could he come up with so many families? Who would want to take more guests?

Jeff started to knock on doors in Meah Shearim. Though there were a few people who took some of his group, most of the answers were more like:

"What? Now? You're kidding, it's a Purim joke, right?"

"I'd love to help, but—"

At one of the doors he knocked on, the family couldn't help him but they suggested he get in touch with the Machlises. Desperate, he called and asked Henny if she could take some guests.

"No problem, send them," Henny replied.

Jeff turned around and saw twenty-five students still waiting to be placed.

"Two students? Three?" he asked.

"How many do you need?"

"Umm... As many as you can take. I have twenty-five students here."

"Send them all!"

That was Henny Machlis. Two, ten, twenty or fifty— her home was open to all.

Henny's Recipes for Life

When a *chesed* opportunity comes knocking at the door you can look at it as a big pain in the neck. *Oh no, another schnorrer.* Or you can look at it the way the *Zohar* looks at it: The Almighty just sent you a gift, a reward to you for being good. What gift? "I'm giving you a chance to help someone."

Remember what it says in the Midrash on Megillas Ruth, "More than a rich person does for a poor person, a poor person does for a rich person."

The walls seemed to expand when they needed more room!

How many guests could fit into their small apartment? It depended on how much space was needed. Rabbi Eli Mayer, a student of Rabbi Machlis and a close friend of the family, remembers the time he was eating a Shabbos meal there. He counted one hundred and forty-seven people, all sitting tightly squeezed together, enjoying the wonderful food and beautiful atmosphere.

When there's love, there's room

Suddenly, there was a knock at the door. There were fifteen people outside, asking to join the Machlis family for a meal!

What would you do if you had a living room crammed with 147 people — and another fifteen guests show up without warning? Here's what happened at the Machlis home: Rabbi Machlis whispered into Eli Mayer's ears, "Pray with me that the walls should expand."

Rabbi Machlis serving the delicious chicken soup

It took a few minutes, but the extra fifteen people were soon seated at the tables. Eli Mayer asked Rabbi Machlis how such a thing could happen. Where did the space come from to fit in so many more guests?

Rabbi Machlis told him, "When there's love, there's room."

Another time, when the house was already packed, *fifty* more people suddenly showed up. Henny didn't panic. Fortunately it was summer. They stopped serving and asked everyone to help move the chairs and the food out to the front yard. People were sent to borrow more tables and chairs from neighbors and presto— the Shabbos meal was eaten outside with enough room for everyone.

Henny never said no to a guest. She had absolute *emunah* that when you're determined to do a mitzvah, Hashem will help.

And she was proved to be right, again and again!

It takes a lot of chicken to feed the hungry crowd!

Henny's special spice

Besides the usual fish, chicken, onions, salt, pepper, sugar and other ingredients that Henny used in her cooking, she added a very special spice: her thoughts and words. She believed that a person's intentions when cooking had a great effect on the food, and on those who ate it. Cook when you're angry and the person eating the food may get hurt. Positive feelings of love, joy and *emunah* while cooking will produce a dish that will elevate and impact the person eating it.

For the eight hours (and sometimes more) that Henny spent in her kitchen cooking for Shabbos the air was always filled with the upbeat music of Carlebach or Shwekey. While peeling vegetables, when adding ingredients, as she put food in the oven or on the stove, the words *lichvod Shabbos Kodesh* — to honor the holy Shabbos — were on her lips. Cooking was done with prayers that those who eat the food should love Hashem and Shabbos. The soup would simmer and the chicken would bake while Henny recited Tehillim.

Volunteers who helped Henny with the cooking remember Henny's words to them as they were crying when cutting onions. "Make the tears holy," she would say. "Cry to do *teshuvah*, cry that the Beis HaMikdash be built and that Mashiach should come!"

Henny had discovered her special spice in the words of Rabbi Nachman of Breslov, who said that when you cook, your emotions go into the food and have an effect on those who eat it. She would tell over how Rabbi Levi Yitzchak of Berditchev's rebbetzin would pray as she cooked that through her food people would want to do *teshuvah*.

Rabbi Machlis had a modest salary as a Torah teacher and Henny's job was full time, taking care and raising their many children. Yet somehow they managed to scrimp and save and in the early years pay for the meals out of their own pocket. They weren't interested in fund-raising to finance the project. The Machlises paid for everything because they felt this was the best way to use their money.

Henny's finances

Sometimes Henny was challenged by concerned family and friends for spending so much money on strangers. She would tell them the story that took place at the end of World War II. The Germans, desperate for money, were willing to be bribed to deliver Jews to freedom at a dollar a head. An English Jew who heard about this

Cooking with Henny was always fun! (Photo credit: Joan Roth)

sold his home and his business to raise $150,000 dollars when the opportunity arose to save Jews from being murdered.

"Do you think the Englishman was crazy?" Henny would ask.

"Of course not. He was saving Jewish lives."

"Well," Henny would then reply, "around us today a spiritual holocaust is happening. So many Jews have no connection to Torah, Shabbos and Hashem. Many are disappearing in intermarriage. I must do everything I can to help Jews find their way back to their heritage. Just like that man in England, I will spend my money to save Jews."

And, yes, many, many not-yet-observant Jews were in fact influenced by Henny's meals to return to Judaism.

That's what she told others. But there were times when things got tough, when there just wasn't enough money to keep her Shabbos hospitality going. That worried her! To have to close their door to guests, to stop doing *hachnassas orchim*, was inconceivable. At times like those she would turn to Hashem and say to Him, "Hashem, this is Your project, please help us." Saying that prayer lifted her spirits and enabled Henny to go on and deal with tough times.

As time went on, some of those who had benefited from the Machlises' hospitality formed an organization to raise funds to help cover costs, which had grown to the enormous sum of $12,000 *a month*. As the years passed the Machlises became famous and hundreds of guests were coming every Shabbos. The expenses became overwhelming, so the Machlises decided to run a raffle. You could win $10,000 dollars at a cost of one hundred dollars a raffle ticket. The raffle and the fund-raising organization were a great help in enabling them to continue their holy mission.

Henny's Recipes for Life

See if you can answer Henny's riddle. You have $100.00 in your pocket and you give ten dollars away for charity. How much do you have left?

Henny's answer is: ten dollars.

Rabbi Machlis at the table, ready for Shabbos

The ninety dollars in your pocket will be spent on toys that break or junk food or clothes that will go out of style. Or you may lose it. However you spend it, that money will soon be gone. Money comes and goes. The reward you receive for giving the ten dollars is eternal, it's yours forever. No one can take it away from you.

Besides the people who walked in off the street, Henny would host entire families as well. In addition to feeding them, Henny had to find places for them to sleep. On those occasions Henny would turn to her neighbors to put up her guests for the night.

Henny's faith

One Friday afternoon a family was expected and Henny hadn't found anyone who had extra beds. Time to worry and be anxious, right?

Not for Henny. Her outlook kept her from worry and anxiety. She faced situations like these calmly. She felt her job was to invite families and do the best she could to find a place for them. But since all her guests are Hashem's guests, it's His job to make it happen. So why worry?

It was getting later and later and Henny still hadn't found a place to put them. Then a neighbor walked in and asked Henny, "Is that your car outside with the door open?" It was. Henny thanked her.

"By the way," Henny asked, "do you know anyone going away, where I can put my guests?"

"Yes," her neighbor answered. "We are!"

So only a little while before Shabbos, Hashem made it happen. Henny's guests had an entire apartment all for themselves.

The very next week it happened again. Henny couldn't find a place for her sleepover guests and Shabbos was coming. Henny, calm as could be, just put her worries and tension on Hashem's shoulders and said, "Hashem, the people coming are Your children, I'm sure You will find them a place to stay." And He did!

This is what happened:

Henny sent her son Dovid to knock on doors to find out if anyone was going away for Shabbos.

Dovid knocked on the first door. No answer. He went to the next door and knocked. A mother holding her two-year-old answered the door.

"Are you going away for Shabbos?" asked Dovid. "We have a family that needs a place to sleep."

"What amazing *hashgachah pratis*! We were already in the car leaving for Shabbos when my little boy decided he had to use the bathroom one more time before we left. So we came back. If he hadn't had to go, you wouldn't have found us home when you knocked. Here, take the keys. Of course your guests can use the apartment."

Once again Henny's faith saved her. Hashem had come through for His children!

Dedication

The legendary Machlis meals took place every single Shabbos. No breaks, no vacations. Week after week after week of shopping, cooking, cleaning and serving meals for so many guests, mostly complete strangers. Even when they couldn't be there because of a family *simchah* or emergency, Henny would cook and have someone come in and lead the meal.

On Seder night there is a special mitzvah for parents to teach their children about the Exodus. The Machlises felt that would be done best if they had only their children with them, so they would go away for Pesach. It was the only time in the year the Machlises' home was closed.

One thing was for sure: the Machlises were motivated! They believed every Shabbos was priceless. Henny believed that feeding all her guests was holy work, a reason for living. After the meals, instead of accepting thanks from her guests, Henny would thank them. She would tell her guests, "Thank you for coming and filling my house with God's presence. The more Jews in a house, the more of God's presence there is."

What made her happy was sharing the joy of Shabbos with others. To Henny, her hours in the kitchen — peeling potatoes, cutting vegetables, cleaning chickens etc. — was her way of giving to others. And when she gave to others, she was behaving like Hashem, the greatest Giver of all, Who provides for all of us. Through her Shabbos cooking Henny knew she was following in His ways, connecting to Hashem, and growing as a Jew.

Henny's Recipes for Life

Henny loved to tell Chassidic stories. One of her favorites was about the Kotzker Rebbe.

The Rebbe was learning with his students and he asked them what they thought was the first great rule of the Torah. Well, it seemed like an easy question. Everyone knows what Rabbi Akiva said, that the great rule of the Torah is *V'ahavta l'rei'acha kamocha,* to love your friend like yourself. And that's how the Kotzker's students answered their Rebbe's question.

But they were wrong. The Kotzker explained that he had asked for the *first* rule. The first rule is: you have to love yourself! You can't treat others with love unless you love yourself first! The second rule is to love others.

Henny would encourage people not to be down about themselves, and not to think of themselves as losers. They should tell themselves how special and talented they are. That there is no one in the entire world that has their strengths and personality. They should say: I'm a winner. I have so much good to do in the world.

Henny knew that when a person feels like a winner they become energized and have the confidence to do *chesed* for others.

One of Henny's greatest qualities was her ability to stay calm when problems arose. It is inevitable that when cooking for so many people something is bound to go wrong. Big or small, Henny dealt with whatever went wrong without panicking or being angry at anyone.

Calm in the face of a storm

Rena was eighteen and a first-time volunteer at the Machlises. Henny had her prepare a rice kugel that would be cut and served to a hundred people. Rena had never made a kugel so large in her life. The size of the pan alone was humongous.

After mixing large amounts of eggs, rice, sugar and oil, Rena poured the mixture into the pan and headed over to the oven. The oven was higher than she was. She had to lift the heavy pan up to get it into the oven. While raising the pan to the oven it tipped over!

What a mess! Rena was covered with raw rice kugel all over her clothes, and the kitchen floor was a total disaster.

Henny looked up at Rena, who was totally embarrassed and feeling awful. Calmly and kindly Henny said, "It's O.K., it's Hashem's will, we'll just make another one." And with that said, she went back to peeling potatoes.

CHAPTER 2

Becoming Henny

There's more to say about Shabbos at the Machlis home, many, many more stories to share. We'll go back to that soon, but now you're probably wondering how Henny became the amazing person she was.

So let's go back in time and travel with Henny on her road to greatness.

A Regular Kid

Henny was a "regular kid," one of five children born to the Lustig family in Crown Heights. She was born on March 13, 1958 (21 Adar 5718). She went to Crown Heights Yeshivah and when her parents moved to Flatbush she transferred to Shulamith School for Girls in Boro Park.

Henny played piano, guitar and loved animals (the Lustigs had a dog). She played Ping-Pong, basketball and tennis with enthusiasm. As a student in Central Yeshivah High School she joined the school's basketball team and the dance club.

What kind of person was Henny as a child? Her family remembers her being outgoing, friendly and a seeker of truth.

Henny meets the Lubavitcher Rebbe

There is one unusual story from Henny's childhood, which happened when she was only four years old. Henny went with her father to daven at 770 Eastern Parkway, the headquarters of Lubavitch chassidim. Though not a Lubavitcher, her father davened there because it was across the street from where they lived.

After davening, Henny and her father joined the others in the shul who were filing past the Rebbe to wish him a good Shabbos. When Henny's turn came, she looked up to where the Rebbe was standing on a platform and said, *"Gutt Shabbos."* Henny was very little, and the Rebbe hadn't noticed or heard her. So little Henny jumped up onto the platform and shouted, *"GUTT SHABBOS!"* This time the Rebbe couldn't help but see and hear the little girl. With a smile on his lips he looked at her and answered, "And *you* should have a *gutt Shabbos.*"

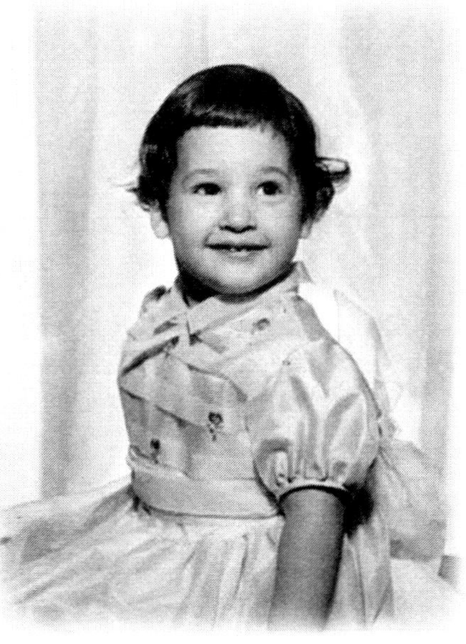

Little Henny, with a big smile

Considering the type of Shabbosos Henny would grow up to have, we have to ask ourselves: Were the Rebbe's words just a coincidence, or maybe a peek into the future? You decide.

Why Worry?

It seems that Henny developed her attitude toward stress and worry at an early age. Just read this poem she wrote as a student facing exams!

Why Worry?
Why worry
Why get sick
With unpleasant anticipation
Will it help the situation?
Why get up tight
Why put up a fight
Why about tests worry
And think yourself a dummy?
If you failed, you failed

And if you passed, you passed
And even if you're sad and fret
It won't change the mark you get.
Well, in my opinion,
(If you want to know)
Worrying will get you no place
Definitely: No, no, no!
If you count your nausea
Or your aching head
Worrying got you someplace—
Right into a sick bed!

The seeds of what Henny would become were planted by her parents, who were themselves outstanding role models of *chesed*.

Henny's parents

Henny's father would bring his Puerto Rican workers to the doctor when they didn't feel

(left to right) Henny's mom Edith Lustig, with her children: Esther, Henny (with the big smile!), Malkie, Chumie, and Yaakov, May 1965

Henny at her sister Esther's wedding. (left to right): Chumie, Malkie, Henny and Esther

well, and her mother always treated the household help, plumber or handyman with respect and kindness.

For a youngster to grow more observant is a challenge. There are many habits that can hold a girl or boy back from growing closer to Hashem. When Henny was young, almost everyone watched television. When Henny realized that TV was hurting her *neshamah* she devised a plan to stop the habit. She promised herself that for every hour of television she watched she would say an hour of Tehillim. It didn't take long before watching TV was for Henny a thing of the past. (Tehillim, of course, became an important part of her life!)

No more!

In her teens Henny had already come to the conclusion that mitzvahs weren't a burden. She realized each mitzvah done was a diamond! Mitzvahs were worth fighting for, worth doing, worth gathering as many as possible.

Reaching out

HENNY LUSTIG

הני

Her voice, like a bell, shall ring forever.

אוהבת את הבריות אוהבת את המקום

"A good humor is goodness and wisdom combined."

עבדו את ה׳ בשמחה באו לפניו ברננה

Henny is lively, spirited and always on the go. Her inquisitive nature and eagerness to learn have resulted in a deep love for Limudei Kodesh. Henny's sincere campaign speech won her the G.O. vice-presidency, and she has been active in the dance and basketball clubs. She is as willing to learn as she is to help others and is thus a sought after friend. Henny's smile and sunny disposition have always brightened our days and brought smiles to our faces.

RESHA ANN LUSTIG

הענא רשא

Henny in her elementary and high school yearbooks. Whoever wrote the captions totally captured Henny's happy, giving and loving personality!

Volunteering for JEP was one of her "diamonds." JEP (Jewish Education Program) was an organization that reached out to Jewish kids in public schools, helping them connect to Torah. Henny would bring home kids who were not religious. Her mother would feed them and Henny would talk to them, sharing with them the beauty of *Yiddishkeit*.

Henny didn't only work with the young. She didn't feel awkward chatting with elderly people either. On Shabbos afternoons Henny would visit the local nursing home, schmoozing with the residents and cheering them up. She didn't forget her family either, and would always walk over to drop in on her aged aunt on Shabbos as well.

During the Yom Kippur war, Henny stood on the corner of Flatbush and Nostrand Avenue collecting money from passersby to send to Eretz Yisrael to help the war effort. Even as a teen, Eretz Yisrael was a place that Henny cared about a lot.

Decisions, decisions

After high school, teens begin to make decisions about what they want to be and what kind of person they hope to marry. These decisions will shape what they hope their lives will be like. Henny was no different, but her choices certainly were! They were different from the choices her friends were making. But that didn't bother her. Henny just walked on her own path.

Children

At eighteen, Henny and her family visited Eretz Yisrael for the first time. Along with all the usual tourist sites, they visited the military cemetery in Yerushalayim, where soldiers who died in battle fighting are buried. Almost all the graves are those of young people in their twenties, soldiers who lost their lives protecting Klal Yisrael. Henny looked out at the rows and rows of headstones and was deeply moved. No, this was not just another tourist attraction.

Henny during her visit to Eretz Yisrael in 1976

Seeing the loss of so many young Jews she decided she would do what she could to replace Klal Yisrael's great loss by having many, many children. Most of Henny's friends dreamed of families with two or three children, maybe four. But from then on Henny dreamed of a very large family. And she fulfilled that dream. Henny had fourteen children!

Mazal tov! Henny and Mordechai at their wedding

Henny fell in love with Torah learning. That was quite unusual when Henny was growing up. Unlike today, very few girls in Henny's age group, including most of her classmates, were interested in marrying a kollel student or someone who wanted to become a rabbi. The ideal husband was someone who could make a good living, someone who might even get rich someday. Boys with degrees in accounting, law or medicine were in high demand.

Finding a shidduch

Not Henny. She knew who she wanted to marry: a *talmid chacham,* someone who loved learning.

She found him. His name was Rabbi Mordechai Machlis. He was a *talmid chacham* who taught Torah and loved Torah as much as Henny did.

In 1979 Henny and Mordechai boarded a plane, leaving the country where they grew up to move to Israel. There they built their life's dream, to live a Torah life in Eretz Yisrael, have a big family and share with others the great joy of Shabbos and Torah. Henny was only twenty-one and newly married.

What's important?

When renting an apartment, most people ask questions like, what condition is the apartment in, are there any leaks, is there enough air and light? The Machlises had one question about the Maalot Dafna apartment they were looking at. How far is it to the Kosel? The apartment was only a half hour walk away, and they took it. The Machlises felt that to be so close to the Kosel was important.

Years later, when they were seeking to buy an apartment in Maalot Dafna, they had other questions. Not how many bedrooms does it have or how large is the kitchen — but how big is the living room. Will it be big enough to fit the many guests they fed on Shabbos?

From the beginning of their life in Eretz Yisrael, what was important for the Machlises was: How close can we be to the holiest spot on earth? And will the apartment be big enough to do the mitzvah of *hachnassas orchim?*

Worry... later

Arriving in Eretz Yisrael, one of the worries this newly married couple had was: How would they earn a living? Rabbi Machlis started looking for a teaching job, going from school to school, talking to principals and leaving resumes. Place after place he was told the same thing, "We have nothing right now. If something opens up we'll call you."

Rabbi Machlis was becoming quite discouraged. It was almost the beginning of the school year and no one seemed to need him. Finally he got a call. It was from Beis Midrash L'Torah, known as BMT.

BMT was willing to give him a chance. But there was a catch. The yeshivah only needed him to substitute for a rebbi who was leaving for a few months. It was an election year in Israel, and the rebbi wanted to work for one of the religious parties. The elections would take place in November. The job they were offering would be to substitute from September to November.

Henny and her mother visiting the Kosel

Rabbi Machlis didn't know what to do. Should he take the job or not? On the one hand, if he takes it, he'll be out of work in the middle of the school year with nowhere to go. On the other hand, if he doesn't take it, he might not find anything else and be unemployed the entire year! So he asked his wife what she thought.

Tough question, right? What would you tell him to do?

To Henny the answer was obvious. She told him, "Hashem sent you a job now, take it. Let Him worry about what will be in November."

So Rabbi Machlis took the job — and he taught in BMT for twenty years! It turned out the rebbi he was substituting for loved politics so much he never came back.

Moving to Eretz Yisrael requires a strong dose of *emunah* that things will work out — and Henny's *emunah* was very strong!

CHAPTER 3

Shabbos With Henny

We promised you more "Henny" stories about Shabbos at the Machlis home, and here they are!

For most of us, the traditional Shabbos food that comes to mind after cholent is gefilte fish — ground-up fish mixed with eggs, matzah meal, a little salt and pepper, and lots of sugar — eaten together with a little *chrein,* horseradish. Yum! It's a fabulous food. But for our Sefardic brothers and sisters, Shabbos fish is supposed to be hot and spicy. In their culture, who ever heard of sweet fish? So when a Sefardic man who was a bit "unusual" encountered Henny's fish, there was quite an outburst!

Extreme... patience

In front of all the many guests who had come to enjoy the Machlis food and hospitality, he got up and demanded, "Who made the fish?"

"I did," Henny answered.

"This is awful! Who ever heard of sweet fish? You can't make fish!"

There was a stunned silence in the room. If this happened to you or me we would have probably gotten angry and thrown the man out for his chutzpah. Henny's approach was different.

Henny said, "You are correct, I can't make fish. Would you teach me how to do it right?"

"I sure will," he answered.

"When?" asked Henny.

"Thursday morning, I'll be back."

With that he sat down and everyone was able to finish their meal in peace.

On Thursday morning, Mr. Spicy Fish showed up to keep his promise. Instead of getting rid of him, Henny stopped what she was doing and let him teach her. He showed her how to cook fish fillets in a sauce of tomatoes, turmeric and peppers, Moroccan style.

That Friday night Henny served sweet gefilte fish — and spicy Moroccan fish.

I bet you think the story is over. Wrong! There's more. Remember, we told you Mr. Spicy Fish was "unusual."

When the fish was served he got up and told everyone, "You know why the fish is good tonight? Because I taught her!"

Henny didn't say a word. She just let him talk.

Sometimes people would ask Henny, "Why do you let crazy people in?"

She would answer, "Isn't everyone a little crazy?"

Without panic

One Shabbos, the Machlises' Shabbos meals were doubling as a *sheva berachos* for a young couple who had just gotten married. The *chasan* was a *baal teshuvah*, who had become Torah observant. His parents, Jews who had unfortunately lost their heritage, were there as well. They weren't exactly excited about their son's new lifestyle choice. To be frank, they thought that religion was a bad thing for their son, and so were their son's plans to learn in a yeshivah.

The Machlises were hoping that good food and *zemiros* would give them a different perspective on religion. The meal was going well but Henny could see disapproval in the faces of the *chasan's* parents. Well, she thought, maybe their attitude would improve when she served the much anticipated savory main dish, Henny's famous cholent. Eating a bowl of piping hot cholent on a cold day would surely bring a smile on their faces.

Henny went into the kitchen to get the pot of cholent. She took the cover off the large pot and was hit by a terrible smell. *Oy vey*: The cholent had spoiled!

Henny went back to the meal, where everyone was waiting for the cholent course to be served, and explained what happened. She told everyone that it was what Hashem wanted. "I'll serve an extra dessert instead," she announced.

While the guests were eating chicken Henny called one of her daughters to come help her in the kitchen. Together they started to prepare the "extra" dessert. They began cutting brownie cakes into squares, and Henny told her daughter to decorate them and make them look fancy. After creatively decorating the brownies with different toppings, Henny's daughter piled them up in the shape of elegant towers on trays. It looked like dessert platters served at a wedding. She placed them on a side table for the guests. Suddenly someone walked by and accidentally swept by the brownie towers, toppling them so that all the brownies fell down over the floor.

Henny's reaction? "Looks like the Almighty doesn't want us to have dessert either."

You may think that by this time Henny's plans to impress the *chasan's* parents with the wonders of Shabbos food had failed completely. Yet the Divine plan was different.

After seeing Henny's reaction — or better said, her lack of reaction — to what had happened, the *chasan's* father told Rabbi Machlis that he had changed his mind about what his son was doing. "If going to yeshivah will teach him to have a giving and warm home like this one, and be able to deal with the challenges of life calmly and without blaming others like your wife does — I'm all for it," he declared.

It wasn't the wonder of Shabbos food that helped the boy's parents accept his choice; it was the wonder of Henny Machlis!

One of the reasons Henny could stay so calm when things got crazy was because her motto was, "Hashem will help." And guess what? He did help — again and again.

Hashem will help

There was the time the Machlises ran out of cholent on Shabbos. When that would happen, which it did occasionally, the Machlises would take up a collection of leftover cholent from the neighbors. But this time the neighbors' contributions just weren't enough. What to do?

Someone came up with an idea: Let's send someone to the catering hall a few blocks away. Maybe they will have leftovers from a Shabbos event. (Jerusalem has an *eruv* and so people are allowed to carry there on Shabbos.) Sounds unlikely, but guess what? That week the caterers had prepared way more than was needed and they had plenty to give the Machlises for their hungry guests.

Cholent always seemed to be the critical issue. One of the key ingredients in cholent is barley. In Eretz Yisrael, years ago, barley had to be checked for bugs. In a family cholent it's no big deal, people had to check a cup or two. But in the Machlises' home, bags and bags had to be checked ***every*** *erev Shabbos*. It was a tedious and time-consuming job, so instead the Machlises would use bags of "bugless" barley; that is, barley that doesn't need to be checked — which friends would bring from the United States.

One of their helpers, Aliza Friedman, was once in their home on Friday, helping out. When she went to prepare the cholent she saw that there was no barley. Worried, she asked Henny, "What do we do now?" The answer was classic Henny Machlis: "Hashem will help."

Time passed, Shabbos was getting closer and closer and still no barley. It seemed it would be a cholentless Shabbos. All of a sudden there was a knock at the door. A young lady was standing there with a duffel bag full of — you guessed it — bags of barley she had just brought from the States!

Henny's Recipes for Life

Henny taught: We should live in the moment. Then we won't feel the pressure of "There's a lot to do."

She didn't mean you can't plan for tomorrow. What she meant is that whatever you are doing, do it with all your focus and concentration. And most important, you should think to yourself, "There is only one thing to do, and that's whatever Hashem wants me to do right now."

Henny would say: Think: Now Hashem wants me to cook. Now He wants me to feed the baby. Now He wants me to shop. Now He wants me to listen to a friend going through a hard time. Now He wants me to call my mother.

At any given moment, there is only one thing that needs to get done. And that is the "now." Don't do it in a frenzy and rush. Do it calmly, with all your attention and energy.

You can teach yourself to think this way too! Feeling overwhelmed? Say to yourself: Now Hashem wants me to study for the Chumash final. Now He wants me to visit my friend who broke her leg. Now He wants me to hike up this hill with my bunk, even though I'd rather be reading a great book.

You'd be pleasantly surprised how much more relaxed your life will be!

Ever notice how your mom's fridge or oven breaks down right before she needs it most? Like just before *Yom Tov* or when she's cooking for a family *simchah*. Well, the same thing would happen to the Machlises, only it happened quite often.

Hot chicken

Once, about an hour before Shabbos, there was a knock on the door of one of the Machlises' neighbors, a woman named Yonina. Batsheva Machlis was standing there. "Our oven broke," she explained. "My mother asked if we could bake this in your oven."

Yonina had finished cooking for Shabbos so she agreed, with a bright smile. But the smile disappeared when Batsheva came up, carrying a deep tray with layers of chicken.

"It's almost Shabbos!" she told Batsheva. "There's no way this will be ready."

"My mother said to put it on the highest heat and not to worry," Batsheva replied.

And indeed, when Yonina pulled the tray out, instead of a batch of half-baked chickens she saw a miracle: All the chickens had come out piping hot and perfect!

It was a Thursday night; no, actually it was already Friday, because it was 1:30 in the morning. Yonina and her husband, the Machlises' neighbors, were walking back from the Kosel to their apartment. The street was dark and quiet.

Chicken tops or bottoms?

Just as they were passing the Machlises' apartment, Yonina's husband turned to her and said, "I wish we had something to eat, I'm soooo hungry."

Suddenly they heard a voice coming out of nowhere, "How about some chicken? Do you like tops or bottoms?"

They saw someone waving to them from a window. "I'll be right there," Moshe Machlis called down to them. He opened the door for Yonina and her husband and invited them in. He wrapped up some chicken and even gave them a bottle of soda to take home.

Yonina and her husband had a great meal. And Moshe? He was doing the Machlis thing, making another *Yid* happy. Just like he learned from his parents.

Henny with Moshe, 2003

And with a more grown-up Moshe, 2014

A man walked into the Machlis home for the Shabbos meal. He was a mess. He looked (and smelled) like he hadn't taken a bath for a month.

Spoon feeding

Yehoshua Machlis greeted the man and led him to a seat. Then he gave him some soup. Problem was, the man's hands were shaking so badly, he couldn't pick up the spoon. Yehoshua, seeing what was going on, sat down next to him and fed him, spoon by spoon.

Henny with Yehoshua

Another amazing thing about Henny was she didn't just cater for the large groups of guests that came her way, she catered for individuals as well. Once, Henny made a salad for fifty guests with salad dressing that was made with mayonnaise. One guest came to Henny and told her, "I don't like mayonnaise." No problem: she went into the kitchen and made him dressing without mayo.

Individuals count

Then there was the woman who didn't want to attend the regular meals. She felt uncomfortable sitting with so many people. Henny would feed her an entire *seudas Shabbos* at two in the morning! Henny not only fed her but spoke with her and comforted her, sometimes speaking with her until four in the morning.

All the guests would get soup with three kneidlach, except for the fellow who would come to the kitchen and insist on having seven. He asked for seven and got it because Henny said, "That's his *oneg Shabbos,* so we will give it to him." The same went for the man who would eat three-quarters of a cream pie all by himself.

Henny's love wasn't just for Klal Yisrael, but for every *individual* in Klal Yisrael as well.

Henny's Recipes for Life

Every person in Am Yisrael has to learn. We also all have to teach. The Lubavitcher Rebbe says, "If you know *alef beis* and your friend knows only *alef*, teach him *beis*."

Impact

A Shabbos at the Machlises' could change a person's life. Just from watching how the family members behaved toward others, their outpouring of *chesed* and warmth, had an impact on guests. The beauty of Shabbos and the words of Torah discussed at the meal often made guests who had negative feelings about Jews or Judaism reconsider their mistaken beliefs.

The Austrian

When the tourist Rabbi Machlis had invited for Shabbos rose to speak, he introduced himself and shocked everyone. He revealed that he was Austrian, and that he was not a Jew. Austria was a nation that had worked closely with the Nazis to murder the Jewish people during the Holocaust. And now here was this Austrian, enjoying Jewish food on the Jewish Shabbos!

The man then proceeded to share with everyone that in the town he came from, the people were taught that the Jews are a bad people, unkind and mean.

He said, "Now I know these are all lies. You Jews are in fact good and kind. When I get back home I am going to tell everyone that what we were taught was a big lie."

That alone would be a great *kiddush Hashem,* but the story isn't over yet. On another Shabbos not very long after this happened, a fellow got up at the Shabbos meal and announced that he was from Austria. He had come because his church's spiritual leader in Austria had said that the Jews were a good people. That what they had heard about the Jews being bad was a lie. "And if you don't believe me," the spiritual leader had said, "go to Jerusalem and visit the Machlises."

The Austrian continued to speak. "I decided to go and check things out for myself, and what I saw here has really changed my mind about the Jewish people."

It turned out that the Austrian tourist who told Rabbi Machlis he would go back and tell everyone how great the Jews were had kept his word. He went back and told all *1200 members (!)* of his church what he had discovered about the Jews in a small apartment in Maalot Dafna.

Wow!

The doctor

Rabbi Machlis had just made Kiddush and poured the wine into small cups to be distributed to the guests. One of the guests, a doctor from Holland, was having difficulty. The doctor's hands were shaking so much he couldn't lift the cup. Concerned, Rabbi Machlis asked him if everything was all right. The doctor explained that his parents were Holocaust survivors who didn't want anything to do with *Yiddishkeit.* "This is the first time in my life I have had a Jewish experience and I'm so excited about it that I can't stop my hands from shaking. I plan on going home and start learning what Judaism is all about."

Where she belongs

The woman who came into the Machlis home with her husband and children was dressed in jeans and a T-shirt. She looked sulky. She really didn't want to be here. Her name was Valentina. She and her husband came from Central America, and she really didn't know why her husband was making her come to this Jewish house.

When Valentina was young, she didn't go to church like the rest of her family. She would say, "It's not my place." It bothered her that she didn't feel at home in church. Sometimes at night she couldn't fall asleep. She would cry to herself and wonder, "Where do I belong? Where do I belong?"

When she got older, she met a man named Matias. The two were married, but she decided not to have a church wedding like her sisters.

They were a handsome and well-to-do couple. Matias was a neurologist and Valentina was a lawyer. They had nice children and it seemed their lives were perfect.

Time passed. Matias came up with an out-of-the-box idea. He told his wife he wanted to volunteer to be a doctor in Israel. It wasn't as strange as it sounded, because deep down Matias felt he was a Jew, because his father was Jewish. The plan was that he would come first, get an apartment and set things up. Then Valentina and the children would join him in a few months.

During the time he was living in Eretz Yisrael waiting for his family to join him, Matias spent Shabbosos with the Machlises. He couldn't wait for his family to come and he was looking forward to bringing them to meet the Machlises on Shabbos.

After his family finally arrived and they had settled in, Matias told Valentina that on Friday night she wouldn't have to cook dinner. They were going to eat at the Machlises.

Valentina was not happy. She didn't know much about Jews, but she knew she didn't like them. "Jews are dirty. They're disgusting. I'm not going, Jews are gross."

Somehow Matias got her to go. When they walked in the Machlises' door, Matias introduced his wife to Henny who gave her a big hug and walked her into the living room.

Valentina stopped short. She stared at the many Shabbos candles flickering and lighting up the room. And suddenly she started to cry. She just kept repeating the words: "This is my place! This is my place!"

After Shabbos, Valentina came to Henny, wanting to learn more about Judaism. Since Henny didn't speak Spanish she brought her to Rebbetzin Hana Simon, a neighbor who did. The rebbetzin started teaching Valentina the Seven Noachide Commandments that a non-Jew must observe.

When Valentina realized that the rebbetzin was teaching her how to be a good non-Jew she interrupted angrily. "Stop this!" she told the rebbetzin. "I want to be a Jew." Of course the rebbetzin calmly and quietly explained that she doesn't have to become Jewish. All God wants from her is to keep the Seven Noachide Commandments. The rebbetzin did all she could to change her mind. Nothing worked. Valentina had found where she belonged: she wanted to become Jewish.

Valentina and Matias (who had learned that though his father was a Jew, by halachah he was not Jewish) stayed in Eretz Yisrael and learned how to be Jews. Two years later they stood in front of the famous Bnei Brak *beis din* of Rav Nissim Karelitz. The Rav talked to them, checking if they were really, *really* sure about becoming Jewish. After speaking to them for some time Rabbi Karelitz remarked that of all the converts his *beis din* had dealt with, these were the most sincere he had ever met.

Valentina, Matias and their three children converted and Valentina and Matias got married as Jews. Who do you think made the wedding? The Machlises of course!

She was Jewish, her husband was German. They had come to Eretz Yisrael on their honeymoon.

Just one Shabbos...

Having heard from other tourists about the awesome experience of eating at the Machlises, they decided to join them for a meal as part of their sightseeing. It would be fun to see the "natives" in their own habitat instead of from a hotel room, kind of like swimming with the dolphins.

It was a Shabbos to remember. More, it was a Shabbos that would change their lives.

After they left the Machlises, the intermarried couple decided they wanted their children to grow up in a home like the one they'd just been in, a home filled with warmth, love and compassion for others.

Two years later the Machlis family got a letter. "You probably don't remember us, but because of what we saw that night we started our return to Judaism. We want to share with you the fantastic news that my husband is becoming a *ger tzedek,* we are keeping Shabbos and all the mitzvahs."

Just one Shabbos can change lives. Especially if that Shabbos is at the Machlis family's home.

Of course the Machlises weren't always successful in changing people's lives. But often, a seed was planted — a seed that might one day turn into a Jew returning to Torah life. Like the seed planted in a woman who was part of a group of Mormons.

The Mormon guests

The Mormons had joined the Machlises at the Friday-night Shabbos table. When it was their turn to speak, as everyone was invited to do during the meal, each of the Mormons in the group gave the Machlises a simple thank-you for hosting them.

Except for the last woman in the group. She stood up and told the Machlises how she was so thankful and excited to have had this chance to experience Shabbos — because her mother was Jewish.

Hearing this, Henny shouted excitedly, "Then you're not a Mormon, you're Jewish! You're my holy sister!"

"I am a Mormon, I am certainly not Jewish!" the woman retorted.

Henny replied, "According to Jewish law you ARE Jewish no matter what you think you are."

The lady shot back, "No, I'm not!"

Henny realized that she might have more luck talking to her privately after the meal. So she just let the matter drop.

But talking to her after the meal didn't work either. The woman left with her Mormon friends.

The next day, on Shabbos, she came back to the Machlis home. With tears in her eyes she told Henny she hadn't slept all night. She was confused. Who was she? "Please, tell me the truth. Am I Jewish?"

"You sure are," said Henny. "One hundred percent Jewish."

The lady stayed for the Shabbos meal— and never came back.

Is she still living as a Mormon? Or did she return to living as a Jew? We don't know. But one thing is for certain: Henny Machlis created a spark that may one day burst into flame.

Don't think that the Machlises' guests were only not-yet-religious Jews, non-Jews, converts and *baalei teshuvah*. The Machlis home was open to *frum* Jews as well. Homesick

And religious Jews too...

sem girls knew they could find a warm home and a good meal at the Machlises; *frum* tourists and yeshivah students loved the atmosphere of *kedushah* (and the cholent!)

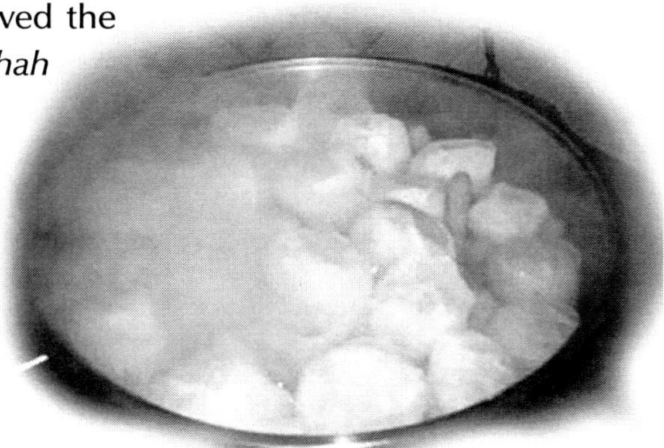
Loaves of love: Gefilte fish bubbling on the stove

And the lonely people were there too: divorced men and women, singles living away from home, widows and widowers — they all came. A Shabbos at the Machlises meant not being home alone. The atmosphere of love and Shabbos joy lifted their spirits. One regular was a broken forty-year-old man who had just gotten divorced and was not allowed to see his children. He became a regular at the Machlises for over fourteen years! He told Henny that their Shabboses made his life worth living.

In the Haggadah, when we start the Seder we invite everyone by saying, "Let all those who are hungry come and eat. Let all those who are needy come and celebrate Pesach."

Rabbi Machlis would ask, "Why do we need the second line? Why invite someone twice? If someone is hungry, he won't come to eat until you invited him twice?"

The answer, he said, is that in the first line the Haggadah is talking about inviting people who are hungry for food. The second line is inviting people who are needy and hungry for Torah, or for love and warmth — for people who are hungry emotionally or spiritually.

No matter who you were or what you needed, the Machlises were there for you.

By now you're probably asking yourself: How did she do it? Was she a *malach,* an angel who never got tired or burnt out? What about her children? With so many guests around when did she give them any attention?

How did she do it?

The answer is yes, Henny did sometimes get

tired of standing on her feet for hours cooking in a hot kitchen. She was a righteous woman but not a *malach*. What did she do when she couldn't take it anymore? Henny would go to the forest, spend some time there and talk to Hashem. She would say, "Please give me the energy to feed Your people. I need Your help. " Taking a break in the forest and praying helped her a lot. It gave her the will and strength to go on. She would come back to her kitchen fully energized, ready to take on the cooking and cleaning once again.

And of course the Machlises paid attention to their children! They would have a beautiful private meal with their kids first, then eat with the guests.

CHAPTER 4

Chesed 24/7

Henny's open-house policy wasn't only for Shabbos. Her house was open during the week as well.

One of Henny's weekday guests was an elderly man with no job, no savings. He was a bit of an odd character in a nice way, and had absolutely no sense of time.

Whole wheat pizza

He would eat supper with the Machlises when they ate, or whenever he showed up, sometimes very late at night. After a few times when he came very late at night — or, rather, very early in the morning! — Rabbi Machlis put his foot down and told him not to come later then 1 a.m. A reasonable request, wouldn't you say? It didn't help. As he told Rabbi Machlis, "I'm a very busy man! I can't commit not to come after one o'clock! "

So the Machlises had to come up with another plan to deal with this guy. (Not taking care of him was not an option.) They told him to come in whenever he wants and just help himself. The door was left open. Henny even taught him how to make his favorite food, whole wheat pizza. She showed him where the flour and all the other ingredients were so he could make it himself.

It was three in the morning when the Machlises were rudely woken from their sleep by a banging on their bedroom door. They jumped out of bed to see what the emergency was. No, it wasn't a child with a tummy ache. And thank G-d it wasn't a fire or flood. It was— you guessed it— Mr. Pizza Man.

"What's the matter? What's going on?" asked Rabbi Machlis.

"I'm hungry."

"We told you, take whatever you want."

"I want pizza and I forgot how to make it. Come out and teach me again."

As you can imagine, Henny's husband Mordechai was ready to hit the roof. Let's face it, no one is at their best at three in the morning. Right?

But Henny, standing by her husband, saw something else.

She saw opportunity.

She turned to her husband. "You know what? This is a test from *Shamayim*. I'll go."

She went out and taught Mr. Pizza Man all over again!

Henny's Recipes for Life

Do you ever judge people? Like, "He is such a nerd/weirdo/loser. I don't want to have anything to with that guy!" The truth is a lot of people think that way. They judge people by how they dress or what they are doing or how they act.

These are the kind of people who walked right past a man playing a violin at a Metro station in Washington, D.C. His violin case was open so that people could drop coins in. He played his heart out for forty-five minutes and collected $32.

His name was Joshua Bell. He was one of the world's greatest violinists, and he was playing on a violin worth $3,500,000! (That's three and a half million dollars, for those who get mixed up by all the zeroes.)

Did anyone notice what kind of magnificent music was being played there? Did anyone care? No! They saw a beggar playing a violin, judged him as a loser and walked on. (If you're wondering why he did it, it was part of a social experiment to see if people would notice. And guess what? They didn't!)

Every Jew, even when he or she is down and out, is a diamond.

A dirty diamond, maybe — but still a valuable gem. If you found a diamond in the mud, wouldn't you pick it up, bring it home and clean it?

Don't judge people by what you see. Instead, uncover the diamond that lies beneath all that mud.

Now don't think that Henny was always the big *tzadeikes* and her husband learned from her what's right. Sometimes it was the other way around. Henny learned a lot from her husband as well.

Worth a lot — but not valuable

We are taught that the tent of Avraham and Sarah had four entrances, so no matter from which direction a traveler was coming they would see an open door, a place where they could rest. Following in their holy ancestors' footsteps, the Machlises decided that they would leave their apartment door unlocked, so that if someone would need to rest they could just walk right in.

One day Henny came home and realized they had been robbed. Some of her jewelry was missing. She was very upset, not only because of the missing jewelry, but even more because someone they had been kind to had taken advantage of their hospitality.

When Rabbi Machlis came home he stayed calm. He comforted his wife and shared with her the idea that it was only jewelry that they'd lost, worth a lot, maybe, but not really valuable. Children, Torah, mitzvahs, guests, all of Klal Yisrael — those are valuable.

Henny got the point. Through the years, as they hosted so many strangers, the rest of her jewelry eventually disappeared, and even her engagement ring. Silver kiddush cups also vanished. But it didn't bother Henny anymore. When her kids would come and tell her about yet another item that had been stolen she would tell them, "It's not stolen, just borrowed."

Don't be ashamed

The Machlises lived the teaching of our sages to go to extraordinary lengths not to embarrass someone. Having so many guests and volunteers helping out in the kitchen, it was inevitable that uncomfortable accidents or situations would occur.

They were masters of patience and cleverness, knowing just what to say or do to make sure that no matter what someone did they would not be embarrassed. The following stories give you an idea of the Machlises' embarrassment-prevention policy.

Mazel tov! Mazel tov!

Alex was enjoying himself at the Machlises' Purim meal. The food was great and plentiful, the guests all in the Purim spirit. But the wine bottles on the table were already empty. When Alex heard Henny ask her husband to go to the car to bring in another carton of wine, Alex volunteered to go instead. Struggling with the heavy carton Alex managed to get it into the house, when— Booom! The entire load dropped out of his hands.

There was wine and broken glass everywhere. Hearing the sudden noise all the guests turned to the source. To Alex. Silence fell as all eyes looked at him. You can imagine how he felt.

After a moment, Rabbi Machlis and Henny both yelled, "Mazel tov! Mazel tov!" Rabbi Machlis grabbed a few guys and Alex found himself surrounded by people dancing and singing. Alex broke out in a broad grin and joined the fun.

The opera singer

One Shabbos, after everyone had enjoyed a lively round of *zemiros,* one of the guests stood up. She announced that she was a professional opera singer and she would like to sing a solo in appreciation for the Machlises' hospitality. This woman had no idea that it is not permitted for a woman to sing in front of men. *Oy*! How could they tell her without hurting her feelings?

Swiftly, Henny walked over to her and told her how delighted she was at her offer. After the meal, she said, they would be delighted for her to give a performance for all the women guests.

Happy ending: The Torah's laws were kept, the opera singer sang and no one's feelings were hurt.

The volunteer in the Machlis kitchen carefully poured a bag of rice into the pot. She noticed a second bag of rice, and cheerfully added it as well.

Oh no!

A few minutes later, Henny walked over. "I'm making a rice kugel," she said. "Have you seen the bag of rice that was on the counter?"

"Oh, no! I put both bags in to cook," the volunteer said, her cheeks flushed with embarrassment. "I'm so sorry."

Henny paused for a moment, then she grinned. "*Baruch Hashem*! Nothing happens in this world without a reason. If you put in an extra bag it means Hashem is sending us more Shabbos guests than I expected. That's wonderful news!"

And another person was left smiling and not ashamed.

Chesed isn't only about feeding people. Sometimes it's about talking to people to lift their spirits or helping them in other ways to get them back on their feet.

The stockbroker

One of Henny's "cases" was a New York stockbroker who had been in jail for conducting business in a way that broke the law. He had done his time and was out of prison. But besides a jail sentence the judge had given him a ONE MILION DOLLAR FINE to pay.

After jail he decided to rebuild his life in Eretz Yisrael. He had been a wealthy man who lived in a fancy house, had his own office, drove expensive cars. All gone. Everything. He had no money, and he owed one million dollars. He'd been a respected man in his community, but now? Respect? Who had respect for someone who had served time in jail?

He was broke and depressed by what he had been through.

Now, in Eretz Yisrael, he met the Machlises. Henny saw that more than food this fellow needed *chizuk*, words of encouragement. Henny talked to him, and talked to him and talked to him some more, persuading, reassuring and convincing him that he could look forward to a great future.

At first he couldn't believe her. "But Henny, I owe a million dollars! How can I ever pay that back? I'll be in debt the rest of my life! Who is going to marry me? I'll be alone the rest of my life."

Again and again he would come to the Machlises for meals and Henny would give him pep talks.

And, finally, he realized Henny was right. He did have a future. He stopped feeling sorry for himself. He found someone very special who accepted his past, didn't mind that he owed so much money, and married him. Henny's sincere words had fixed a broken man.

Henny's Recipes for Life

Of the many ways there are to be *b'simchah*, to be happy, Rabbi Nachman of Breslov teaches that the very first way is to smile.

Smiling is a good activity. It releases certain hormones, called endorphins and serotonin, in your blood. Having more of these hormones in your body makes you feel happier and helps your body fight diseases. So practice smiling — it's good for you!

One of the other ways of being *b'simchah*, Rabbi Nachman says, is to think about what life will be like when your problems are solved and don't exist anymore. Imagine how happy you will be, and then bring those feelings of joy into the present.

After Henny passed on, when the Machlis family was sitting *shivah*, a chassid with a long coat and long *payos* walked in. His story was astounding.

The chassid

"When I first met Henny, I was an angry and bitter young man. Long hair and earrings, that was me. I had stopped being religious. I was so lost that I was going to marry a non-Jew! Henny was determined to stop me. I don't know how she did it but she persuaded me to break off the planned marriage. Thanks to her my children are Jewish and I exchanged my long hair for *payos* and my earrings for a chassidic coat."

Henny's Recipes for Life

Henny used to say: "If a Nobel Prize winner falls in the mud, isn't he still a Nobel Prize winner? Of course. He just has to clean the mud off." That was Henny's attitude when reaching out to people who had been raised in religious families and who had left keeping the mitzvahs. They were still special people; they just had to clean the mud off!

Let's dance

How do you get someone who is depressed out of bed? That was Henny's challenge when she visited a family whose mother was unfortunately suffering from mental illness. The woman mostly stayed in bed all day, sad and gloomy. Except when Henny showed up. Henny came with an assortment of really good jokes to tell. The two of them would start laughing together at Henny's jokes. Then Henny helped the woman out of bed and they would dance and dance and dance until Henny had to leave. The family was amazed at how Henny's magic helped their mother.

Henny believed that if she heard about a person in trouble, lonely, poor, depressed or with *shalom bayis* problems, it was a message. A message from the Almighty meant for her ears, asking her: What are you going to do about this? Almost always Henny found a way to help.

Ten seconds of *chesed*

One of Henny's favorite Torah thoughts was from the *Zohar*. It teaches that not only will a person suffer for hurting others with their words, but they will also suffer for any good words that they could have said to someone, and didn't.

A few words that take only ten seconds to say can change a person's day. Wherever Henny went she left good feelings behind with her "ten-second *chesed*."

The beggar

Some people who see a street beggar walk right past him. Others drop a coin in his cup as they walk by, without making eye contact, treating the beggar as if he were invisible.

And Henny? When she would pass someone asking for charity, she would give them a coin, and then talk to them as well. She'd share a word of encouragement, a smile, or a comment like, "What a beautiful purse you're wearing." The beggar would smile back and maybe sit a little straighter. What a difference ten seconds can make!

***Sheva berachos* Torah**

Henny's sister-in-law, Rebbetzin Mashy Shatzkes, remembers that when Henny would meet Rebbetzin Shatzkes's husband she would always mention how much she'd enjoyed the *dvar Torah* he had said at her *sheva berachos.* Henny would even quote portions of his speech — which he'd said thirty years before!

The cop

How about a good word to someone who just made you miss your bus or bumped into you and caused you to drop the money you had in your hand down the sewer. That would be tough, right? Not for Henny.

Once, she was driving on the highway when in her rearview mirror she saw those dreaded flashing lights that means a cop wants you to pull over.

Henny pulled over to the shoulder of the highway, the cop right behind her.

A policewoman got out of the car and asked for her license. "You were driving in a bus lane," she said sternly, "and I'm going to have to ticket you." Henny was shocked; she hadn't realized that she was driving in the wrong lane.

Now no one likes a ticket, it's expensive and annoying. Most people tend to become angry at the cop, even though she is just doing her job.

What did Henny do? She told the policewoman that it was her birthday and that she wanted to give her a blessing that she should get married soon. And she gave her a few other blessings as well.

The cop never wrote the ticket!

We may wonder: Did Henny treat her own family with her amazing patience and *chesed*? Perhaps she was so busy being good to others that she didn't remember that her own kids need a good word too?

What a mess!

Absolutely not!

A Machlis daughter remembers calling her mother after she was married and crying to her that she was not coping with the housework. She felt overwhelmed by the dirty dishes, the floor that needed washing and the laundry piled up all over the house.

"Ima told me it will all be O.K. The house will get clean. Just talk to Hashem and say, 'I need help, I'm not good at cleaning and housework. Please Hashem make the house look nice and neat again.'"

Henny's daughter followed her mother's advice. She told Hashem her troubles and then, amazingly, she found the strength to tackle the mess.

"A bit later I looked around. The mess was gone! Ima's advice had done its magic!"

Another daughter remembers the times her mother would come visit her in Ramat Beit Shemesh. Even if the house was a mess her mother would say, "The house looks great, you did a spectacular job! It looks like you just had a cleaning lady here."

Henny's Recipes for Life

Imagine that the Chafetz Chaim just walked into your classroom. Wow!

He sits down and begins teaching. Suddenly he notices that his shoelaces are untied. He is old and frail, and he can't bend down to tie them himself. He looks up and asks, "Can anyone here help me tie my shoes?" You and all your friends fly out of your seats and race to go and help the *tzaddik*.

So why is it that when your little brother comes to you and asks you to tie his shoes or help him get dressed, you say, "Not now," or "Stop being soooo annoying," or "Go ask someone else"? Why would you do *chesed* for the Chafetz Chaim and not your brother? His *neshamah* is holy, just like the Chafetz Chaim's. Remember: Doing *chesed* for your family or any other Jew is as great as doing it for the *gadol hador*!

Saraleah Dershowitz, Henny's niece, needed to have surgery to deliver her baby. She was scared. Hearing about how afraid she was, Henny came running to help. She gave her niece a speech she will never forget.

Aunt Henny to the rescue

"Hashem loves this baby and wants it to be healthy," Henny told her. She reminded her niece that it was Hashem Who was in charge. "Say, Hashem take all my fears and worries."

Henny continued with her comfort and advice. When Saraleah was taken in for the operation, Henny told her, "Close your eyes and imagine Hashem giving you a huge bear hug."

And, of course, she promised her niece that she would be waiting outside, davening for her.

Henny's words hit the mark. Because of them, when Saraleah went to the hospital she wasn't nervous or afraid. She felt Hashem's "hug" and her aunt's warmth and concern. And she delivered a beautiful baby!

Henny with her niece's newborn baby

We can do *chesed* even if someone is far away. That's why telephones were invented! All kinds of people from around the world would call Henny with their problems, to get advice or because they were lonely and needed to talk to someone. No matter who it was, Henny gave them her attention and gave them *chizuk*.

Faraway *chesed*

Sometimes she would get the whole family to help people. She would put the caller on speaker and say something like, "Joan is lonely." Then the Machlises in the room would shout together, "We love you, Joan. We all wish you were here."

The Shabbos meals were *chesed* the Machlises did once a week. Henny and her phone did *chesed* every day, at any hour of the day.

Henny's apology

Often people would call when they were insulted or hurt by someone else. They would be full of anger and resentment, and sometimes they wouldn't only complain about the person who'd done something wrong, but also about all the people who dressed like him or her. Say they were driving and got stuck behind someone who had parked illegally. If that inconsiderate driver had long *payos* and a long black coat they would complain about all chassidim. Or if someone wearing a black hat pushed to get onto the bus, then all yeshivah guys were ill mannered, rude and didn't keep the mitzvahs of *bein adam lichavero*.

How do you get these people to calm down? How do you get rid of their anger and resentment against everyone religious because they were hurt by the actions of one person?

You can't do it by defending them. Try that and they will only get angrier. So Henny found a unique way to deal with them.

Henny would apologize.

She would say, "On behalf of the yeshivah world, I apologize. You deserve much more respect. The Jewish people are what we are only because of the yeshivahs." Or, "On behalf of the whole religious world, I apologize. It was a mistake. We didn't mean to hurt you. If you really knew the religious world, you'd appreciate how good we are." Or, "On behalf of all chassidim, I apologize. We shouldn't have treated you like that. If you knew chassidim personally, you would love them."

Henny would end with: "Please, do you accept the apology?"

How did Henny come up with this idea? From reading *Mishlei*, her favorite book of Tanach. There it says "a soothing tongue is a source of life" (15:4), and "pleasant words are like a honeycomb, sweet to the

A *sheva berachos* in the Machlis house for one of their guests

soul and healing to the body" (16:24). Henny worked hard on training herself to speak sweet and pleasant words. Eventually it became her nature to talk that way.

The night before surgery is a time of tension and worry. All the patient wants to do is rest and try to remain calm until they enter the hospital and are wheeled into the operating room.

The wedding

On Thursday morning Henny was scheduled for surgery to remove her cancer. Even though her family begged her not to, she insisted and spent all day Wednesday shopping, cleaning and serving a wedding meal that took place at her house Wednesday night. Even the *chuppah* was her responsibility, taking place in her front yard under the stars. From Henny's point of view she was preparing herself for surgery in the best way possible. She knew that making a wedding for someone would enable her to bring one more wonderful mitzvah with her into the operating room to protect her during surgery.

A newly arrived Russian immigrant with no family in Israel and no place to live was looking for a place for Shabbos. He was told to go to the Machlises.

Russian hospitality

When Henny heard that he had no place to live she invited him to stay with them. He didn't leave for quite a while. How did he express his gratitude? When he came back from getting his new Israeli identity card, with a big smile on his face, he proudly showed them his card. The Machlises were quite surprised to see their name on his card. It turned out that he was so thankful for what the Machlises did for him that he officially changed his last name to Machlis!

Mazal was a poor Israeli woman who would come to the Machlises for meals every so often.

Mazal's fish

"I haven't eaten for days," Mazal told Henny piteously. "And I want so much to eat *dag charif.*"

Well, you know that Henny loved to give people the food they liked, but as it happened Henny couldn't give Mazal *dag charif*, which is fish cooked in a very spicy sauce that Sefardim love. She had none of the ingredients in the house.

She offered to make her pasta. No. Eggs, bread, salads, schnitzel — whatever she had in the house. But Mazal insisted she would only eat *dag charif*.

While Henny was negotiating with Mazal to eat something else (tuna? mashed potatoes? avocado salad?) there was a knock on the door, and in walked the Machlises' Sefardic friend and neighbor, Mrs. Lari, carrying a plate of *dag charif*!

"I cooked too much fish, much more than I need," she explained. "Can you use some?"

So Mazal got her delicious meal — and the Machlis family had still another example of the *hashgachah pratis* that was so often found in their home!

Imagine having a friend sit *shivah* in your home. For an entire week people are coming and going at all hours to visit the mourner,

***Shivah* home**

who is sitting in your living room. They are all strangers to you. For a whole week your home has a heavy cloud of grief and sadness. It's a hard job, but the Machlises did it.

A young Italian woman whose father was a non-Jew but whose mother was Jewish had been attracted to her people and started to learn about what it meant to be Jewish. Then she decided if she really wanted to pursue the truth she should come to Eretz Yisrael to study *Yiddishkeit*. She joined a seminary for *baalei teshuvah* and eventually became Torah-observant. She even persuaded her mother to come, and she, too, became *frum*.

Unfortunately, some time after coming to Eretz Yisrael her mother was diagnosed with a terrible disease and after a few months she passed away.

This young woman has just lost her mother. She has no home in Eretz Yisrael other than her dorm room in seminary which she shares with four other girls. She is a *baalas teshuvah,* alone and on her own. Where can she sit *shivah*?

Where? The Machlises, of course. For this Italian *baalas teshuvah* the Machlises turned their small apartment into a *shivah* home.

Not only did Henny face life with an attitude that she had all the time, space and money in the world, she also saw herself as having all the strength in the world.

Hot soup

Getting out of bed is so hard to do. Imagine you've gone to bed, all tucked in under your blankets, warm and cozy. There is a knock on the door. You just know it's someone asking for a handout or maybe kids in the building asking for food for an organization that helps poor children. Do we have the strength to get out of bed and answer the door?

Henny did.

It was a freezing cold Tuesday night. Henny had made soup for supper and after feeding the family she had gone to bed.

A while later she heard one of her daughters answering the door. Someone had come by for soup. From her room Henny heard Tamar telling him that they had no hot soup, but he was welcome to their leftover cold soup.

Henny yelled out, "It's cold outside. He needs HOT soup. Wait just a minute; I'm coming out." She got out of bed and warmed up the soup.

When the Machlises were out and couldn't answer the phone, even their answering machine spread good feelings and joy to the caller. This was the message they would hear, in both Hebrew and English:

Even when no one was home

"*Shalom u'vrachah* from the Machlis family. Thank you so much for calling. May Hashem bless you in ALL that you do, with the highest levels of happiness, good health and success. May all gateways of blessing be eternally open for you and yours. And may you be blessed with a long, healthy, happy and sweet life, with no difficulties or stress. May this day be the greatest day of your life so far. And may tomorrow be even greater."

Where does greatness come from? Having a clear set of priorities and goals. Understanding in your heart and mind what is important.

In Henny's own words

Here are Henny's thoughts, taken from one of her notebooks.

What inspired me to persevere in chesed:

1. *"B'tach Ba'Shem v'asei tov—Trust in God and do good." (Tehillim 37:3)*
2. *Don't do what you can do. Do more than you can do.*
3. *When we do chesed, we bring more chesed into the world.*
4. *The Tanya says that you get help from Heaven when you decide to do something, not when you're just thinking about it.*
5. *When Hashem loves you, He sends you a present: guest to your door.*

CHAPTER 5

How She Did It

So how does a normal person, just like you and me, turn herself into a *tzadeikes?* It comes with hard work — and only a small step at a time.

Henny wanted to grow and she believed that life wasn't given to us to *only* have a good time and take it easy. We are supposed to enjoy life, but we have to invest our time and effort into growing closer to the Almighty. From her teenage years till the day she died at age 57, Henny kept putting one foot in front of the other, determined to become a better and better person. That is how Henny did it.

Climbing Everest

Henny strived for perfection. She was always trying for more and more, and she was never satisfied with the spiritual level she had reached. She knew that if you aim for perfection, you will either get close or actually achieve it. If your goal is to climb Mt. Everest, you may or may not reach the peak, but you will climb pretty high. Higher than you ever thought you could.

It's the same with *avodas Hashem* and *middos.*

Henny's daughter Tamar once visited Rebbetzin Batsheva Kanievsky, and was totally inspired by what she saw. She came home and told her mother that she wanted to grow up to be someone like Rebbetzin Kanievsky.

Her mother's response? "You will be."

Tamar said, "But I'm so far from that."

Henny told her daughter: "If you want it, one day you'll get there."

That was Henny's way of doing things. She *wanted* to become what she became, so it happened.

That doesn't mean there won't be times when it will seem impossible or times when you will fall. But that's part of the process. It's to be expected. A *tzaddik* falls many times before getting there.

As Henny's daughter Yocheved once said, "The people who are in the fitness classes are the thin people. The people working on themselves are people who are already aware. My mother wanted to bring her *middos* to a high level. It's exactly because she was so aware of giving everything over to Hashem that she noticed there were parts of her life that weren't given over to Hashem. When she wasn't perfect it bothered her. She was always trying to perfect herself."

Rabbi Machlis testifies that his wife was always searching for ways to get closer to God. Her connection got stronger and stronger as the years went by. Toward the end of her life she reached the level of recognizing that everything around her is all God — *ein od bilvado* — there is none but Hashem.

She'd climbed her Everest!

Torah and Mussar

To accomplish her goals, throughout her life Henny looked to the words of Torah and *mussar sefarim* for inspiration, and to Torah teachers for guidance. In her college years Henny learned *Sefer Derech Hashem* with a chavrusa. As a young mother in Eretz Yisrael Henny had a chavrusa in *Chovos HaLevavos,* and she also met with the women in her neighborhood to learn the halachos of *lashon hara*. She constantly attended *shiurim*. Among those she went to regularly were those given by Rav Chaim Pinchas Scheinberg, Rebbetzin Fruma Altusky, Rav Zev Leff, Rebbetzin Tziporah Heller, Rebbetzin Leah Kook, Rav Zelig Pliskin and Rebbetzin Tzira Morgenstern.

Why and how did such a busy mother find the time? Let's hear what Henny herself had to say about her Torah learning: "By trying to attend two or three Torah classes each week, learning Torah helps me combat my *yetzer hara*."

Henny realized that we need guidance on how to take the *mussar* lessons we've learned in books and apply them to everyday modern living. So Henny would attend seminars and *mussar* classes where proper responses to real-life situations were discussed.

For over ten years Henny belonged to Rabbi Leib Kelemen's Mussar Vaad, which works on *middos* according to the teachings of Rav Yisrael Salanter and Rav Shlomo Wolbe. She also joined the teleconferences of the Personal Growth Chabura of Rav Aryeh Nivin of Ashdod, filling many notebooks with notes from the *chabura*. She was such a great mom, and yet she was always on the lookout for ways to become a better parent by attending long- term parenting seminars.

Henny's Recipes for Life

This was one of Henny's favorite Torah thoughts that she'd heard from Rav Zev Leff.

The Gemara tells us that Rabbi Shimon bar Yochai learned in a cave for twelve years. When he finally came out he saw people busy with their work and their everyday activities. It says that everywhere he turned, his holy fire burned up whatever he looked at. He said, "These people are leaving eternal life and are busying themselves with things that don't last." Immediately, a Heavenly voice proclaimed: "Have you left your cave in order to destroy My world? Return to the cave!"

Rav Leff asks an amazing question. "If Rabbi Shimon was so great that he couldn't relate to the everyday world, why did he have to go back to the cave to study for another year? You would think Heaven would tell him, 'Hey, you're too intense. Go to Florida, put your feet up on a beach chair. Chill out!' Why did HaKadosh Baruch Hu say to go back to the cave?"

So Rav Leff answers, "If people criticize other people, it's not because they learned too much Torah; it's because they didn't learn enough Torah. They didn't learn enough Torah to understand that everyone has their own way of how to serve Hashem, on their own level. That's what Rabbi Shimon bar Yochai had to learn that year."

Henny not only grew and pushed herself but when she found something that would bring joy and inspiration to others, she spread the knowledge.

Take a card, take a book

She went to Rav Zelig Pliskin's Happiness Workshop and would carry around his "Happiness Cards." These were printed cards with fun suggestions such as, "Smile at the mirror, and it smiles back at you." Henny would hand the cards to friends and people she knew.

When she read the book *The Garden of Emunah*, which is all about trusting Hashem, she loved it. She took forty copies of the book in her luggage when she flew to New York for her mother's birthday celebration. In New York she gave the books to her cousins as gifts.

Someone asked Tamar Machlis at the *shivah* for Henny, "Was your mother born perfect?"

Born perfect?

"I told her that wasn't what made my mother great. My mother always said, 'I'm a growing person.' She was great because she worked on herself. And that's what she did till the end of her life."

In an excerpt from one of Henny's notebooks we catch a glimpse of what her goals were, in her own words:

Vision Statement

To know Ein Od Milvado. To be doveik in Hashem always. To love Him and think of Him.

To be calm, spiritual, happy, positive, appreciative, sensitive, honest, focused, GRATEFUL.

In Henny's mind Hashem wasn't just there when she prayed or needed something. She was aware of Him all the time. In everything she did. Even when she tried to lose weight.

Henny went on regular diets and some unusual ones as well. She tried the "watermelon diet" and the "sprouts diet," always searching for the one that would really work well. Besides dieting, Henny walked with her husband or with one of her children to help her lose weight as well.

Ask anyone who is dieting and they'll tell you the greatest challenge is when you open the fridge and there is this really yummy-looking cake staring you in the eyeball. At that moment every dieter asks themselves, "Should I eat it? Or shouldn't I? It looks soooo good! Yeah, but you're trying to lose weight!" When Henny went through this kind of test, when it's oh-so-hard to resist, she would say, "Hashem, help me!" She drew her strength to resist from a higher power than herself.

One Shabbos morning Henny came down to her kitchen and there on the counter was this incredibly rich and delicious-looking cake, a creamy, luscious mousse cake. All the voices inside her started to talk, telling her all the reasons she shouldn't eat it. "It's not healthy, eat an apple instead." "Think of the calories!" She tried and tried but by eight o'clock in the morning she just couldn't resist anymore. It disappeared into Henny in a matter of moments.

Of course, right after she had eaten it Henny was disappointed in herself because she hadn't done what was right. She had let her desire for cake get the better of her *neshamah*. Eating or not eating was not just a question of dieting. It was a spiritual struggle of not over-indulging in food; of letting the mind rule over the desires, rather than the reverse.

She felt so bad about what happened that she apologized to Hashem. That morning, at 11 a.m., she did *hisbodedus,* where a person goes to a quiet place and speaks their heart out to Hashem. "Ribono shel Olam," she said, "I'm sorry. I fell, but please don't be so far from me. You know I didn't really want to do it. I just fell. I'm human and this is how we are. I'm sorry." This was Henny's *teshuvah*.

Later that week a person who was becoming Torah-observant came to visit. He'd been *frum* for a while. What he told Henny was amazing!

"Last Shabbos morning," he said, "at 8 o'clock, I just couldn't stop myself, I just had to text someone. Whenever I did that in the past I would feel like it's all over, I'm not really *frum* and I will never be *frum*. I give up. I would take off my *kippah* and I wouldn't keep Shabbos for the rest of the day.

"But last Shabbos was different. I can't explain why, but even though I had texted at eight on Shabbos morning, by 11 o'clock I found the strength to go to shul. There I prayed to Hashem and told him, 'Hashem, You know I love You, and I don't know what happened. I just couldn't help myself, I texted on Shabbos. I'm sorry.' Then I kept the rest of Shabbos, even taking time to learn some Torah."

The "coincidences" of the times between Henny's actions and this *baal teshuvah's* were perhaps amazing, but not surprising to Henny. Henny believed strongly that all Jews are connected to one another and what we do has an effect on those we are connected to, particularly our friends and family.

Now there's something to think about next time you want to do something wrong or right. It's not just about you; it's about your brother, sister, parents or friends. How will what I do affect them?

Rav Usher Freund *zt"l*

Henny had learned this idea from a rebbe of hers, Rav Usher (pronounced Ooh-sher) Freund. She was very close to Rav Usher, and he had a big influence on her life.

Rav Usher Freund

Rav Usher was a *tzaddik*, chassid and a

Jerusalem legend. The Tolna Rebbe said about him: "He was the Baal Shem Tov of our generation." Rav Usher was known for his extraordinary acts of *chesed*, putting up the poorest and most broken people in his apartment. And Henny Machlis certainly followed her Rebbe!

Henny's Recipes for Life

Rav Usher Freund used to say that when our thoughts aren't positive ones, we are flooded with sadness. So just say, "I'm happy now." For that one second, feel happy. Feel the joy of one second of breath Hashem gave you when you inhale, and say, "I'm happy this second." A second of happiness is important, even if the next minute you won't be happy.

CHAPTER 6

Growing Up Machlis

What's it like growing up in a house that has a hundred guests every Shabbos? What's it like having parents who are known as the Avraham Avinu and Sarah Imeinu of our time? I can tell you this: It's certainly different from growing up in a regular home.

Elisheva, the Machlises' second-oldest daughter, remembers the excitement when the family got a second table for their dining room. "We danced around the new table, because we were doing the mitzvah of *hachnassas orchim,* welcoming guests. My father was singing loudly and my mother, who was expecting, was dancing with us kids around the table. It's a beautiful memory."

With so many guests, were the Machlis children forced to spend their time cooking and cleaning and serving? Absolutely not. Henny's policy was never to force her children to help, unless they wanted to. And guess what? Most of the time, they wanted to!

Much more than diapers

When Henny had her twins she had four kids in diapers. Not easy! Henny was having a hard time coping. Rabbi Yehuda Samet had heard that things were a bit chaotic in the Machlis home, so he dropped by to give Henny some encouragement.

He told her how when he and his wife also had several small children in the house, they put up a sign over the changing table that said, "I AM CHANGING THIS DIAPER IN ORDER TO HELP THIS CHILD

Ima Henny: Henny with Yocheved and Elisheva, her first two children.

GROW INTO A *TALMID CHACHAM*, A *YAREI SHAMAYIM*, AN *OVEID* HASHEM, AN *EISHES CHAYIL,* AND I'M DOING IT WITH SINCERITY AND JOY."

From then on Henny was able to cope, inspired by the importance of what she was doing when she was changing diapers.

Cheer up!

When the Machlis kids were having a hard time, Henny taught them not to come complaining and kvetching. Instead, they should ask, "What can we do that will cheer me up?" Some kids would ask for an iced coffee, others would want to go to the Kosel and some of the kids would want to dance to music. Instead of feeling sorry for themselves, they learned to cope with challenges and keep a positive view of life.

"One of a kind"

Henny's son Eliyahu was her twelfth child. That's a lot of older siblings for a kid to have and since some of those siblings were married, that's also a lot of nieces and nephews, all taking attention away from him.

Except that they didn't, because Henny made sure each of her kids got the attention they needed. For Eliyahu, that meant that she drove him to and from school each day, a half-hour trip, even

Henny and her "one-of-a-kind" Eliyahu

though he could have taken a bus. When he left the car, she would call out to him from the window, "You are special, you are one of a kind."

And speaking of "one of a kind": at the time of Eliyahu's bar mitzvah Henny had a bad case of cellulitis on her foot. (If you don't know what cellulitis is, you're lucky; it's a tremendously painful skin infection. Ouch.) Instead of moaning and groaning, she put on her fancy high-heeled shoes and danced and danced. And though it took her weeks to recover from that evening, she assured Eliyahu, "It was worth it for your bar mitzvah."

And that is totally a one-of-a-kind mom.

What's the problem?

At one point in her life Henny was worried if all her efforts on behalf of the Jewish people might be wrong, because they were taking so much time away from her own children and husband. Should she stop the Shabbos meals and focus only on her family? So she went to the *posek hador*, the great and revered Rav Elyashiv, for an answer.

He told her, "I don't understand your question. There are seven

Henny, Mordechai and some of their kids at a visit to a chocolate factory.

days in a week. Six days you give to your family and the seventh day you give to Klal Yisrael. What's the problem?"

Nowadays, most people who live in the Yerushalayim neighborhood of Maalot Dafna keep Shabbos. It wasn't always like that, though.

The Kids' Kiddush

When the Machlises moved in, there were many families who were not religious.

What to do to help their neighbors? On Shabbos, the Machlis kids would go out and yell, "Kiddush, Kiddush, any kids who come get cookies." Many children heard their first Kiddush at the Machlis home.

When Batsheva Machlis was in fifth grade, a girl in her class was very mean to her. Batsheva told her mother, "Ima, she's so bad."

Befriending the bully

Henny told her, "Don't hate her. Just be nice to her, because she's probably going through her own stuff." Because of what her mother said, Batsheva worked on being friends with her, even though no one else in the class was friendly with this girl. They became close. One day the girl told Batsheva her secret. Her parents were divorced, and she had a hard life.

Henny always taught her kids, "Hurt people hurt people." She meant that people who are feeling hurt themselves tend to lash out at others.

Bedtime stories

When the Machlis kids were small, in the early 1980s, there were few Jewish children's books. Yet Henny refused to read them children's stories like Cinderella, Snow White, or Bambi. Instead, she created her own books, with stories from the Torah and Gemara. She would draw pictures of camels and robed figures, and bind the pages together in book form. Instant kosher bedtime stories for her kids!

Henny believed that her children would absorb holiness from what they are exposed to. So besides reading them only Jewish books, she often put her babies out on the back porch in order for them to hear the sounds of Torah learning coming from the nearby *beis midrash* of Yeshivah Ohr Somayach.

The car crash

One of Henny's sons got into twice as much trouble as her other kids. You know the kind of kid I'm talking about. He's the one who is always getting sent to the principal's office. Mister Hyperactive Mischief Maker. To protect his privacy we'll just call him "Son," O.K.?

Once, when "Son" was thirteen, he got into a car crash. Do they let kids drive so young in Israel?, you probably want to know. Well, the answer is NO!

This is what happened. "Son's" aunt and uncle had come from America to celebrate his bar mitzvah. He went to visit them in their hotel room. His uncle gave him the keys to his rented car and asked him to please bring up something that he'd left there.

"Son" went down in the elevator to the hotel parking lot. He found the car, opened it and couldn't resist the temptation to drive the car! *Baruch Hashem* he came out without a scratch, just shook up a bit.

But he managed to smash three cars in the lot and he totally totaled his uncle's rented car!

When his uncle found out what happened, of course he immediately called "Son's" mother. You can use your imagination as to what happened when Henny got there, but you would be WRONG!

Henny gave her son a big hug, calmed him down, and said, "It's O.K., it's only a car, it's only money. Everyone makes mistakes. Don't worry."

WOW!

"Son" had caused $10,000 worth of damage. The Machlises were told if they told the car rental company that "Son's" uncle was the one who smashed up the car, everything would be covered by insurance. They wouldn't have to pay a penny. All that was needed was for them to say a little lie.

Henny and Rabbi Machlis wouldn't do it. Truth was sacred. You don't lie, even for ten thousand dollars.

Instead, all of "Son's" bar mitzvah gifts went to pay for the damage.

Eventually "Son" grew out of his mischievous antics, and today he channels his active nature into keeping the Machlis hospitality going.

In 1999, Henny gave birth to a baby boy. He had something called infant jaundice, which gave his eyes and skin a yellow tinge.

Get me to the bris on time!

Though infant jaundice is not usually serious, if a baby boy has infant jaundice his bris is delayed until the jaundice disappears, since giving a jaundiced baby a bris can be dangerous.

To find out if the baby had jaundice or not, the baby's blood is tested for something called "bilirubin," which causes the yellow color of the skin. If he has a bilirubin count of more than 12, he can't have his bris. The parents wait till the count goes down, and as soon as it does, the baby gets his bris.

Henny's heart was set on fulfilling the mitzvah of having the bris on the baby's eighth day, which according to halachah is very important. But a blood test on the baby's seventh day showed that he had a bilirubin of 16. That was way too high for a bris the next day, which is what the doctor told Henny.

"What do you mean, there'll be no bris on time?" Henny replied. "Today is only the seventh day. Let's see tomorrow."

The next day, when her son was eight days old, she took the baby for another blood test. The bilirubin had gone down to 14, still too high.

The doctor said, "So now you know there's no bris today?"

Henny was stubborn. "What do you mean? It's only 8:30 in the morning. Sunset today is at 5 o'clock. We have till 4:30 to see if his bilirubin goes down."

The doctor had had enough of this lady. "Do you know how long I'm working in this field? The bilirubin will not go down to 12 today. It doesn't happen. It won't happen."

Henny replied, "I'll come back in the afternoon, and we'll do another test."

The doctor told her he wouldn't permit another test, it would just be a waste of time.

Henny would not give up. Though she was still recovering from giving birth, at 2:30 p.m. she took the baby in a cab to a Jerusalem suburb half an hour away, where she knew she could get another blood test done.

The results? You guessed it! The baby's bilirubin count had miraculously dropped down to 12!

The baby had his bris right on time!

Yocheved's wedding

A wedding is a great *simchah,* but for the mother of the *kallah* who has to get all the children dressed, greet the guests, make sure everything goes smoothly, work with the photographer for family pictures and take care of a million other little details, it's also an exhausting affair.

Yocheved Machlis was married the night after Yom Kippur. The family hosted fifty guests who arrived in Eretz Yisrael from America to take part. The wedding was on Thursday night. Friday morning, Henny was up bright and early preparing for the Shabbos *sheva berachos* that would be taking place in her home, which would include all the guests who had flown in for the wedding and THE USUAL HUNDRED STRANGERS who would show up.

Henny and Mordechai at Yocheved and Avraham's wedding

Helping the *kallah*

Henny and her husband didn't always have the money to give to those who turned to them for help. Once, a girl named Hodaya got engaged. Both she and her *chasan* were orphans, and they didn't have money for the wedding expenses. Hodaya's sister and brother in-law turned to the Machlises to help out. Unfortunately, at the time the Machlises didn't have any spare money to give. They left the Machlis home empty handed.

One day, who shows up at the *kallah's* house? A daughter of the Machlises, with an envelope in her hands. Hodaya opens up the envelope and surprise number 1: there's a lot of money in it. Surprise number 2? The Machlises hadn't sent it!

When the Machlis daughters heard Hodaya's story, Batsheva Machlis wrote letters to raise money for her, and she got her sisters to write letters too. They raised three thousand dollars!

When the parents couldn't help, the kids got it done.

Hashem takes care

The special Heavenly eye that seemed to watch over Henny watched over the rest of the family as well. When Leah Machlis was fifteen she wanted to go to camp for the summer. She applied to be a counselor but she didn't get the job.

Her father reassured her, "Don't worry, you'll have a good summer."

Rabbi Machlis called the director of a popular summer program that brought girls to Eretz Yisrael from the United States. The camp provided six weeks of touring and brought in top Torah lecturers to speak. It was a fantastic program, but it didn't come cheap: it cost $4000 per camper, far too expensive for a family like the Machlises, living on Israeli salaries, to even consider.

When the program director heard that it was the famous Rabbi Machlis on the phone, he said, "You do so much for Am Yisrael. No problem and no charge." Leah and her twin sister went for two summers and later her two younger sisters also joined. And they had a blast!

The Machlises were taking care of Hashem's children and Hashem was taking care of their kids!

Here is another example of how Hashem bestowed special gifts on the Machlis children:

Free travel

One day, a not-yet-religious woman visited the Machlises' home. Yael Machlis entertained the new guest. While they were talking, Yael mentioned that she had always dreamed of going on a family trip to Uman, in the Ukraine, to daven at the *kever* of the great *tzaddik* Rebbe Nachman of Breslov — something that was only a dream, because the family couldn't afford to make the trip.

The woman asked how much a trip like that would cost. Yael shrugged her shoulders and said, "It depends on how many of us go."

"How much would it cost for everyone in your family who wants to travel to go?" asked the woman.

Yael thought a minute. "I figure about $2500."

Yael almost fainted when the woman told her, "You'll have that amount in your bank account next month."

She left and the Machlises never saw her again. Her first visit was her last. But she will always be remembered by the Machlises as the woman who sent the money that enabled them to make their dream

Henny at the *kever* of Rav Levi Yitzchak of Berditchev

trip. Henny and six of her children happily flew to the Ukraine for a 48-hour trip. They not only visited the graves of Rebbe Nachman, but were able to pray at the graves of Rav Levi Yitzchak of Berditchev, and the Baal Shem Tov as well.

The best way to teach

One of Henny's children wasn't davening with proper *kavannah*. How did Henny take care of it? Instead of trying to change her daughter, she redoubled her own efforts to daven with *kavannah*. She said, "If I daven with *kavannah*, my children will also daven with *kavannah*."

HAPPY BIRTHDAY!

Many people celebrate their birthdays with friends or family. Some even get gifts. But not all people are so lucky. Imagine how tough it would be if it was your birthday and no one knew or cared. In the following story Moshe Machlis acted on his mother's saying, that when someone tells you something it's a message from Hashem, meant for your ears. You're hearing it because He wants you do something about it.

Standing in the entrance hall of the yeshivah in Yerushalayim where Moshe Machlis learned was a middle-aged man. His hand was outstretched, and he was jingling a few coins in his palm: the universally understood (at least by Jews) action which means please give me something for *tzedakah*.

As he prepared to leave yeshivah for the day, Moshe gave the man some money. They chatted for a few minutes, and the man mentioned that it was his sixtieth birthday. Being a Machlis, Moshe had a great idea. He went over to some of his friends and asked them to join him for a birthday party.

"For who?" they asked him.

"You know the guy that hangs out collecting outside the yeshivah? He's sixty today."

"Cool." "Amazing." "Go for it!"

Moshe and his friends surrounded the collector and told him that they wanted to celebrate his birthday.

"Let's go to a restaurant, you can order whatever you want. We're paying!" On the way they got really into the spirit of things and bought party hats and balloons. They also picked up more friends.

This fellow, who had no one to mark such a special birthday, his sixtieth, wound up celebrating it with twenty people wearing party hats! All because Moshe Machlis listened and understood that Hashem wanted him to hear.

Moshe

At the collector's birthday party. Moshe Machlis is wearing the white shirt (and the party hat!)

and those who joined him made a party none of them would ever forget. What a wonderful gift to receive and what a wonderful gift to GIVE!

Mazel tov!

The Machlis children had an aunt and uncle who had three children. But then the blessing of having children stopped for them, and eight years passed while they waited for another child. One of Henny's daughters felt really bad about the situation, and she decided to pray for her. There is a special, powerful practice of praying at the Kosel for forty straight days, and that's what she decided to do. Day after day, no matter how busy she was or what the weather was she went, for forty days! And guess what? Within a year her aunt had a new baby girl!

Henny, of course, was thrilled when the baby was born. She was so happy for her brother and sister-in-law, who wanted a child so much. And she was delighted that her daughter had learned the lessons of the power of prayer: When you want something from God, ask Him!

The gold bracelet

Henny taught her children to put their faith in Hashem rather than in their own efforts. You can do whatever you want, and plan whatever you want, but without faith in Hashem it's not going to happen just because you wanted it that way. Put God in the picture. Do what you can, but don't try to control everything. Only He is in control. Not us.

Henny would tell her children, "We don't have the best of locks on the doors and we don't have bars on some of the windows. When you're afraid of robberies, daven to Hashem that everything should be safe. We have a neighbor who had a robbery even though she has bars and locks, and I have siblings who had all their jewelry taken by cleaning help. Don't worry, just daven that your things should be safe."

Once, one of Henny's daughters didn't listen to her mother's advice. She had a gold bracelet that was very precious to her because her grandmother had given it to her. It meant a lot to her.

Henny's daughter was very worried that with all the strangers that came through their home it would be stolen. She did everything she could think of to make sure her gold bracelet would be safe. She put it into a box, inside another box, and that inside a bag, and then she hid it under a bed.

One day, when she went to take it out to wear — you guessed it— it was gone. She went crying to her mother. "I didn't listen to you. When I hid it, I said, 'Now nobody's going to get it.' I didn't say, 'Hashem, please watch over it. Now it's gone!'"

There was nothing wrong with what she did to protect her bracelet. But she had not realized that what she did was not enough. Only His help would keep her valuables safe.

Henny's Recipes for Life

Rebbe Nachman said the reason Hashem gives you a scary thought is so you should turn it into prayer. Use it as an opportunity to connect and communicate with Him. If your fear is that somebody's going to break into your house, say, "Hashem, keep my house safe. It shouldn't be broken into ever. Whether the door's locked and alarmed or not, I and my kids should always be safe. Please protect my house."

When you've said enough prayers, then you won't have that fear anymore.

Henny taught her kids to turn to Hashem first and then do *hishtadlus,* practical efforts to help yourself. To do it the other way around is an insult to Hashem. It's as if you're treating Hashem as second best. You're turning Him into plan B. "Hashem if what I do doesn't work out, plan A, I have plan B, You make it work out."

Second best

One of Henny's daughters really didn't "get it." She wasn't convinced, till this happened to her.

In the last year of her life Henny traveled to America for treatments and surgery. For each trip she chose one of her daughters who would go with her and help her, taking care of all her medical and physical needs. Before one particular trip, one of the girls asked if she could have the honor of going. Henny told this daughter that she loved and had very deep feelings for her, but for various reasons she wanted a different daughter to come along with her instead. If that other daughter couldn't make it, then she would be the next choice. Of course, though Henny had spoken to her with compassion and kindness, this daughter still felt rejected, hurt. She left the house.

A few hours later she came back home and gave her mother a strong hug. She said, "Ima, now I understand Hashem. Now I truly feel His pain. I was so hurt because I felt like I was second best. So I went to daven to Hashem, because you always taught us never to blame a person for your pain. I didn't want to blame you for hurting me so I asked Hashem why you wouldn't let me go and I tried to figure out the reason for my hurt.

"Ima, I think I found the lesson in my pain. Hashem waits and longs to hear from us. But if it's a medical problem, first we go to the doctor. If it's a money problem, we go ask others to help us. Whatever the problem, we always look for answers with other people. When that fails we turn to Hashem.

"But Hashem doesn't want to be second best. He's in so much pain watching people turn to everyone else first before coming to Him."

Elisheva Machlis remembers that their mother always encouraged them to look deeper. "Whenever I was facing a big decision, she would always say, 'Elisheva, what does Hashem want from you? Try to see what Hashem wants from you.'"

Hashem wants us

Henny tried as much as she could to get across the message to her children that Hashem wants us to be close to Him. Of course He wants our speech, mitzvahs and Torah. But Hashem also very much wants our broken hearts. He wants who we are, He wants us.

Henny's Recipes for Life

When educating children we shouldn't tell them, "You're so smart, you're so pretty, you're so good and you're so sensitive." You should say, "Hashem made you so smart. Hashem made you so pretty. Hashem made you so good. Hashem made you so quick, so helpful."

That way they will learn not to take the credit for themselves for their accomplishments and achievements. Rather they will thank Hashem for the opportunities and talents they received.

The Machlis family took a trip to the Kinneret, a sea in Eretz Yisrael. Henny took a stone and threw it into the water. Then she asked her young son Eliyahu, "What do you see?"

The invisible stone

He said, "I don't see the stone anymore."

Henny answered, "Don't tell me what you don't see. Tell me what do you see."

"I see the ripples."

Henny told him "Every mitzvah we do may go under the sea, but really it creates ripples and more ripples, and those ripples keep on going. And eventually one mitzvah changes the whole world."

Among the many guests who crowded into the Machlis apartment one Shabbos was an American student studying in Hebrew University. He wore a nose ring and another ring in his eyebrow, and every time Rabbi Machlis spoke about Torah, the student would interrupt, "That's stupid!" or "That's so dumb!" or he would laugh out loud. Really not nice.

A seven-year-old gets the job DONE

Rabbi Machlis remembers him as "the most obnoxious guest we've ever had. During the whole meal, for two and a half hours, he was making fun of everything I said and about what was going on. I told Henny in the middle of the meal, 'I'm going to the bedroom. I can't go on running the meal.'"

Henny and Mordechai surrounded by some of their children and grandchildren

Henny encouraged her husband to keep at it. She said, "Ignore what he says. Don't speak to him; speak to his *neshamah*."

Rabbi Machlis went back in. Finally, after the meal, the obnoxious student left. As he walked out the door, the Machlises' seven-year-old son Moshe asked him, "Why do you have that dumb thing in your nose?"

The student answered back with a question, "Why do you have that dumb thing on your head?" pointing to the young boy's yarmulke.

Moshe answered: "Because I always have to know that there's Someone above me and better than me. Now why do you have that dumb thing in your nose?"

The student went back to his dorm room and wrote in his diary: "Just imagine—that little kid knows why he's wearing a yarmulke, but I have no idea why I'm wearing a nose ring."

On Sunday morning, the obnoxious student came back to the Machlises' apartment, and said, "I'm so sorry for what I did Friday night. I really thought it over a lot. My comments and my remarks were out of place." He added, "I haven't put on tefillin since my bar mitzvah. I want to do something religious to show you that I'm really sincere.

Can I put on tefillin?"

Two years later, the Machlises heard from him that, as a graduate student at UCLA, he was organizing a daily minyan!

Moshe's comment got the job done.

Henny's Recipes for Life

It's O.K. to be honest with ourselves and not to run away from our imperfections. To tell the Almighty, yes, I admit I'm not perfect in this or that. Not to think of ourselves as someone we really aren't. When we admit to ourselves who we really are, we can turn to Hashem and ask for His help, both in *gashmiyus*, physical matters, and in *ruchniyus*, spiritual matters.

That's the reason that we have faults. To connect to HaKadosh Baruch Hu. Reach out to Him and say, "Hashem, if You don't help me close my mouth, I'm going to eat everything in the house. Hashem, if You don't help me close my mouth, I'm going to talk *lashon hara* about every single person I know. Hashem, if You don't help me not to be jealous, I'm going to be jealous of every single person in the world."

Efrat is Henny's youngest. She was her fourteenth child, a special child. She has Down syndrome and is also autistic.

A special child

With the birth of Efrat, Henny met a new level of suffering in the world, which hit her very strongly. This was the first time she had a child who was very low functioning. Dealing with Efrat was challenging for Henny, but she grew to understand that Efrat was the biggest gift. This child she would raise not for her own pride and *nachas* but purely to take care

Playing with Efrat

Henny and her mother at Efrat's Bat Mitzvah in Camp HASC

of the holy soul Hashem had entrusted to her. A visitor who'd spent some time in the Machlis home said to the Machlis children: "I have never seen a mother who loves her child as much as your mother loves Efrat."

So what was it like to grow up a Machlis? Here's what Henny's daughter Yocheved had to say:

Ten shekels of love

The most building, loving experience for me was my mom's unconditional love.

She gave her whole neshamah and full heart to us, even when she didn't have the money to give us more. When my mom taught in Ramat Beit Shemesh, where I live, she would come over every Sunday after she finished teaching. That was the best part of my life.

She would give me ten shekels to buy an "icekafe" [Israeli-style iced coffee], and she would say, "In this ten shekels is all my love. And I wish I could give you all the houses and cars and everything you need. But this is for 'icekafe' for you and I'm putting all my love into this."

Then she would give each of my kids two shekels and say, "This is for you, with my whole heart." After she passed away, my children would say, "Remember the two shekels Savta would give us with her whole heart?" When I think about my mother, her heart, her endless giving meant the most to me.

Henny with her son Dovid and her mother "Boobie" at the Kosel

CHAPTER 7

Happy Henny

Henny had the gift that many of us wish we had: the gift of being a happy person. But the truth is, being happy isn't a gift. It is something a person works on becoming.

Happiness was one of Henny's outstanding characteristics. Here are some examples of what people said about her.

Devora Kovack spent almost all her time in the Machlis house after her two years of seminary. She remembers that in all that time she never saw Henny unhappy. She may have been tired, having stayed up all night, but in the morning she did whatever had to be done with a smile on her face.

Speaking about Henny, Rebbetzin Rena Tarshish said: "Whoever knew her, knew that she was the happiest person anywhere. She always walked around with a smile."

Nothing made Henny happier than babies!

Jokes helped Henny be a happy person. She loved them. She collected jokes from others and made other people happy telling them over.

Jokes

There were the jokes she would start her seminary classes with like: *"What comes out when you squeeze an orange? Juice. What comes out when you squeeze a shul? Jews."*

Another favorite was: *"What do you have when you put a lock on a Torah? A safer Torah."*

One of the hardest times for someone to be happy is when they are sick, suffering in a hospital. It's even harder if they know they are sick with an illness that has no cure. Yet even then Henny managed to lift her spirits and find something to be happy about.

Sad but happy

A few weeks before she died, she said to her daughter Yocheved, "To be happy we always should think about someone who has less than we do. I was trying to think who would want to be like me, sick with a cancer that has no cure yet. And I realized that I just heard about someone who is a father of ten children, who died of cancer. And I realized that he would have LOVED to be in my position—still alive and able to daven. I'm so lucky!"

Henny was a remarkable woman! And don't forget she wasn't born remarkable, she spent a lifetime becoming remarkable. And happy.

On Israeli buses, total strangers will be very straightforward with you and give you advice which you didn't ask for or comment on your behavior. It isn't unusual for teens to be told by a total stranger that smartphones or smoking isn't good for them, or for an old woman to tell a young mother the best way to hold her baby. It's because everyone on the bus is Jewish and we all feel like family.

The bus ride

Once, Henny was sitting on the bus and smiling. Suddenly a young woman sitting next to her started up with her. "You're smiling as if the world is a perfect place," she said. "What about all the hunger in the world, the terrorist problem, the threat of nuclear war?" This woman went on and on, listing all the world's problems and demanding how could Henny sit there and be so happy? When she finally stopped to catch her breath, Henny looked her in the eye and told her, "I'm happy because the world is a beautiful place to live. We have health, we have sunshine and we have water."

Henny's Recipes for Life

Henny used to say, "Your face is public property." What she meant was that everyone could see if you are smiling or crying or angry, and you don't have to share those emotions with the whole world. If something was causing Henny pain, no matter how sad or upset she was, she still always smiled. Her face was public property, but her emotions belonged only to her.

Change the channel

Do you sometimes ask yourself, "How can I be happy? I have so many things to worry about. All I can think about is my mean science teacher, my aggravating little sister, my horrible looks. I can't possibly be happy."

Sure you can. Just follow Henny's advice. All you have to do is…

"Change the channel. You're thinking about this problem and that problem. Just change the channel. That will get you out of it. Talk about what's good in your life. Channel 2 is sad. Let's try Channel 4."

Stay happy

Henny's insistence on the importance of happiness had a powerful effect on her children and students. It helped them avoid depression and sadness even after her passing.

Leah Machlis remembers how guilty she felt after her mother's death. For numerous reasons, she hadn't been able to help her mother as much as her other siblings did. Most devastating of all, she hadn't gone to her mother's last birthday party.

Leah lived in Beitar, and the party was in Beit Shemesh. She had no car, and getting there was very difficult. On top of that, the party wasn't going to start till eleven o'clock at night and so would end very late (it actually ended 3:30 a.m.). Leah had been up since six in the morning, and a late-night party was just not in her plans. She decided not to go.

Turned out she was the only one of the children who wasn't at the party, and unfortunately it turned out to be her mother's last birthday party. Looking back Leah felt bad that she hadn't remembered the teachings of Rav Usher: "Go where Hashem sends you. You have your plans, but He has His plans." She realized she should have gone!

Her feelings could have turned into a serious guilt trip, with sadness and feelings of depression, but Leah decided not to take that path. She was Henny's daughter. She was a Machlis. For her mother's sake she tried really hard to be happy instead. She knew her mother wouldn't have wanted her to be sad.

(However, to do *teshuvah* for not being there for her mother as she feels she should have, Leah visits her father often.)

The dream

After Henny passed away, one of her students decided that for the merit of Henny's *neshamah* she would be happy on Shabbos. No matter what had happened during the week, when Shabbos came she would smile and force herself to think happy thoughts. Everything worked out fine until the Friday she got a phone call five minutes before Shabbos. It was her boss calling to tell her she was FIRED! She was suddenly miserable, anxious and worried about her future.

When she lit the Shabbos candles a few minutes after the call, she remembered what she had promised to do for Henny. It was like a switch went off in her brain and over Shabbos she was happy.

That night, after Shabbos was over, she had a dream. In her dream she saw Henny smiling down at her. When she woke up she felt that Henny had rewarded her for being happy.

CHAPTER 8

Holy Eyes

Henny had holy eyes. She trained herself to look and see the good in people or any situation. Though aware of the bad in people, she chose to magnify the good she saw and let it define the person or situation. This is a trait called *ayin tovah*, a good eye. An *ayin tovah* sees the positive and ignores the negative. A "holy eye" ignores people's shortcomings, whether they are selfish, critical, mean or unfair. Even if a Jew has no positive qualities, they are worthy of respect because they have a holy soul that gives them life, and because they are descendants of Avraham, Yitzchak and Yaakov.

The snowstorm

Snow in Jerusalem! It doesn't happen often but when it does it's exciting. The holy city covered in a blanket of pure white is a sight to behold, like a Jew in his *kittel* on Yom Kippur. Kids make snowmen with yarmulkes on their heads and snowwomen wearing scarves or hats!

A good snowstorm also means the city is cut off from the rest of the country. When there's snow on the ground the roads into and out of the city are closed. No one gets in and no one gets out.

Now *that* was a big problem for Henny, because a snowstorm hit Yerushalayim on the Friday before her oldest grandson's bar mitzvah. He would be called up to the Torah that Shabbos, in his hometown of Beit Shemesh — about an hour's drive from snowbound Yerushalayim!

Imagine you call a grandmother who is about to miss her grandson's bar mitzvah because of snow and you ask, "How are things going?" You would probably get an earful: life is awful, what a bad break, this awful, horrible snow — but when Henny got a call that Friday from one of her Shabbos guests, David, he still remembers her answer. "Everything is wonderful. On Shabbos my grandson is getting bar mitzvah and there's snow in Yerushalayim, it's beautiful!"

Yes, even the inconvenient snow got Henny's "holy eye"!

The day the pipe burst

One time David walked into the Machlis home. It looked like a tornado hit it. There was water all over the floor, the furniture was all out of place, pushed together against a wall. The house was what they call in Eretz Yisrael a "*balagan*." (An incredible mess!) David, concerned, asked Henny, "What's going on, is everything all right?"

Her answer? "*Baruch Hashem*, a pipe burst, and the Baal Shem Tov says where there is water, there is *berachah*."

Inspired by Henny

Baruch relates how he used to live near a "minyan factory." That's a shul where every half-hour or so another minyan gathers to start davening. When he would come for the earliest Minchah of the day, Baruch would pass the people who were just finishing their "morning" prayers. The late daveners disturbed Baruch. Every time he saw them he thought, "What a bunch of lazy people, they probably didn't get up till ten! How can they waste their lives like that? How can they daven so late? They missed the proper time to say Krias Shema and didn't even say Shemoneh Esrei on time!"

Until one day, he stopped being critical of the late minyan. What happened to make him change his mind? His relationship with the Machlises.

He began thinking about what he was doing and he realized that that he wasn't looking at the late daveners with an *ayin tovah*. Henny would look at it so differently, he realized. She would probably say something like: "Look, it's so wonderful to see the Almighty's children talking to Him. It makes me so happy."

And with that thought, Baruch stopped being annoyed by the sleepy guys in the late minyan.

Henny's Recipes for Life

Whether you're doing a mitzvah, studying for a test or changing your baby sister's diaper, do it with happiness! See the positive in what you're doing *("The baby will finally stop crying.")*.

We learn this from what Hashem did after creation. It says (*Bereishis* 1:31) *"Vayar Hashem es kol asher asah, v'hinei tov me'od* — And Hashem saw everything He had made, and behold it was very good." It sounds like Hashem is complimenting Himself. *Look at this world I built, it's absolutely marvelous, I made it Myself.* That's ridiculous! It can't be what the *pasuk* means! So what is it trying to tell us?

The Almighty is saying, "I created a wonderful world. It's your mission to enjoy it."

Say it's raining outside. We can say, "This is terrible. What a miserable day it's going to be." Or we can say, "Great, look how pretty the rain is when it's coming down, and see, our car is finally getting washed!" It's all up to us.

As you're reading this you may be thinking to yourself, "Yes, it would be totally awesome to enjoy the world and be happy, but I hate when Mom asks me to wash the dishes." Well, here are some of Henny's recipes to work on the *middah* of developing a positive attitude about washing dishes, but it can be applied to whatever you're doing in life.

1. The power of suggestion: Say to yourself, I'm going to feel so good when the dishes are done. I'm doing *chesed* for my family.

2. Music: Change the atmosphere inside you by playing music when you're doing something you don't want to. By the time

the playlist is done, so will the dishes. Instead of being angry the whole time, you will have enjoyed listening to your favorite songs.

3. Reframe: What was special about the Mishkan or the Beis HaMikdash? The presence of Hashem that was there. In fact, because we do so many mitzvahs in our homes, every Jewish home is a holy place where Hashem's presence rests. You would jump at the chance to be the one who washed the floors of the Beis HaMikdash, so why not enjoy and be proud of the housework you're doing in the mini-Beis HaMikdash of your home?

It will take time, but following Henny's recipe will eventually create in you a positive attitude toward life about everything! You will enjoy living!

CHAPTER 9

Gratitude, Honesty, Torah and Other Good Stuff

What's the most powerful weapon a person can use to stop being sad? Gratitude. Henny's kids remember when their mother was in a bad mood she would sing, "Thank You, Hashem, for my eyes. Thank You, Hashem, for my husband. Thank You, Hashem, for my children, for my siblings, for feeling strong."

What's remarkable is that she sang that song even when she was sick and in pain. She once told her son Eliyahu, "Whenever I'm in a bad mood or in pain, I always try to think of all my blessings, especially my children."

Henny's Recipes for Life

A clever child knows that if he wants another piece of cheesecake he will say, "Mom, no one makes cheesecake like you. It's the yummiest. You're a great mom. Can I have another piece, please?" And yes, he is going to get another piece. Mom knows very well that her child is using flattery to get another piece. But she also knows her child appreciates her and that makes her want to give him more.

Hashem is our Father in *Shamayim*, and when we thank Him for what He has given us, when we show our gratitude, then in return Hashem wants to give us more. In addition, our gratitude creates a closer connection with Hashem, and that is our reason for living.

Henny avoided making statements that were false. She taught her kids, "Don't cheat to get a better grade, it isn't honest. If it means you get a low mark or even a zero, that's okay with me. What I don't want you to do is lie about it."

Absolutely true

Henny practiced what she preached. Take the following story as an example:

Henny had a television in her home. It was used once a year, when the family watched the annual Tanach contest held in Yerushalayim. If there was a war going on in Israel she would watch it then too, to know what was happening. All other times the TV sat unused in a closet.

The television

When Henny went to register her daughter in Bais Yaakov they asked her if she had a television. Henny explained that she had a TV that she used only once a year, and actually it had been broken for quite some time, but they just never got around to fixing it.

Well, the school administration was not happy to hear that. They told Henny they were going to have to think about whether to accept her daughter and she should come back again for another meeting.

On the way home Henny met a neighbor. The neighbor asked, "How are things going?"

To which Henny answered, "*Oy*, what a day! I just came back from Bais Yaakov and they're upset I have a TV."

Henny then told her neighbor the whole story.

The neighbor said, "Henny, your TV doesn't work. Why didn't you just say you don't have one?"

"Oh, I couldn't do that. It's not one hundred percent true, I have a TV; it just doesn't work."

Henny's Recipes for Life

Most people think *sheker* is when you lie, and if you tell the truth it's not *sheker*. Wrong. Truth can be *sheker* as well, if it's speech that Hashem doesn't want someone to say. Call someone mean, ugly or dumb. It may be true but its *sheker* because Hashem doesn't want you to hurt someone else with the power of speech He gave you. On the other hand, when you lie about a *kallah* and say, "Isn't she the most beautiful *kallah* you have ever seen?" — that's *emes,* that's truth!

We see this in a Gemara that tells us what to do when someone who bought a pair of shoes asks you what you think of them. They are wearing the shoes, which means they can no longer return them. You think the shoes are gross.

You have two options. You can answer the question honestly and make them feel bad, or you can tell them the shoes are stunning. Which should you do? The Gemara answers, tell them whatever makes them feel good EVEN IF IT'S NOT TRUE.

You may be asking yourself: Well, what about "*Midevar sheker tirchak,* Distance yourself from falsehood"? Rav Zusha from Anipoli explains that this means that using words the wrong way will distance you from Hashem. Saying things that will make people feel good has the opposite effect: those kind of words bring you closer to Hashem.

We've said it before: Henny was not born a *tzadeikes*. She worked very hard on herself to get to the high levels she reached.

Controlling her anger

She was always happy, always smiling, but you know what: Henny did have a temper. Here's what Henny's daughter Yocheved said about her mother:

"When we were younger I remember Mom yelling at us, 'What's taking so long?!! Come on, come on.' She had quite a temper. But after she yelled at us she would say out loud, "Hashem, please help me to not scream. Hashem, please help me to not get upset."

Did Henny's children respect her less because sometimes she lost it? Not at all!

"We learned from Mom that it's normal not to be perfect in how we behave. We just have to work on ourselves to get better, just like she did. By the time my younger siblings were born my mother had stopped yelling at the kids."

Have you ever heard of the word "*eepuk*"? It means to hold yourself back, to restrain yourself, not to react when something gets you very angry.

The power of "eepuk"

Say you walk into your room and you see that your little brother has ripped to pieces the picture you'd been working on for days, and you stop yourself from saying all the things you are burning to say (you also don't beat him up). Congrats! You've just shown "*eepuk*."

How long would it take you to say all five books of Tehillim? Two hours? Four? A few days? According to Rabbi Frank, every time you show *eepuk* — even just for a few minutes — you have accomplished more than you would have by reciting all of Sefer Tehillim.

Rav Nachman of Breslov also talks about this. When you came in and saw your little brother making confetti out of your masterpiece, you were just tested by Hashem. Showing *eepuk*, passing the test and not saying anything, has the power to bring to you whatever you were hoping for. Whether it was being accepted into a certain high school or yeshivah, or for a sick relative to get better, or even for a shidduch, learning to show *eepuk*, to hold back from opening your mouth and responding negatively, is a great skill to have.

You ask, "How can I keep quiet when I'm so infuriated or upset with someone? It's impossible!" As hard as it sounds, it can be done. Henny had four steps she used to train herself from responding in anger.

*Think!: We are not on the level of the Noam Elimelech, who said that before saying something a person should think it over thirteen times. But we can ask ourselves before we speak, "Should I say it?" When we're upset, disappointed or angry, we should think, "Hashem, should I say this? Is this what You would want me to say?"

* It's Him: Remember: if there's a mess-up Hashem has let it happen. If it isn't Hashem's will, it wouldn't happen. It could be a test to

see if we react the right way, or it could be for our benefit somehow in the long run. For instance you miss your plane because your brother who was supposed to drive you to the airport overslept and picked you up late. What aggravation! Boy, are you upset at him. But it turns out that the plane was hijacked. It's all Hashem and He knows what He is doing. So why scream and yell at the situation?

When someone messes us up and we get angry, think over and over, "It's You, Hashem." Because when we are focused on thinking or muttering under our breath, "It's You, Hashem," we can't yell or argue or criticize others at the same time!

**Korban Todah*: A *Todah* was the name of the offering brought in the Beis HaMikdash when a person wanted to give thanks to Hashem for surviving a life-threatening situation; to say *todah*. So when your little brother spills his ice cream on your brand-new suit, don't yell. Say: "Thank You, Hashem, for giving me a little brother who is so cute." Too hard to see how cute he is right now? What about: "Thank You, Hashem, for giving me such a good family and a nice place to live in." Don't just see the inconvenience you are suffering from right now; look at the whole picture and be thankful.

*Daven: Pray that Hashem gives you the strength not to get angry. If we don't ask for His help, we won't get it.

When Henny's nephew Rabbi Eliyahu Dershowitz was nineteen years old Henny asked him to run some errands for her on *erev Succos*.

Oy, I forgot!

She wanted him to buy challahs and wine and a few other foods. Most important of all, she asked him to pick up her husband Mordechai's suits from the cleaners. Before Yom Tov, she told him, they had given in every one of his suits to be cleaned, and if they weren't picked up he would have nothing appropriate to wear for the entire holiday, since the dry cleaners were closed the whole week of Succos.

And — you guessed it! — Eliyahu forgot.

Let's let Eliyahu tell the story: "When I got back with the groceries, of course the first thing my aunt asked me was, 'Eliyahu, did you bring the suits?'

"All I could say is, '*Oy*, I forgot!' And all Henny said to me is, 'It's O.K.'

"'I'll go back and get them,' I said. Henny said, 'Don't bother, the cleaner is closed already.'

"That's it! I couldn't believe it. I didn't get yelled at and my aunt didn't panic, she kept her cool. I was amazed at how much self-control she had! It was *gadlus*.

"Many times I saw people yell at my aunt and she never lost it. She would just take it. When I asked her how could just stand there and get screamed at without reacting, she told me, 'Why get upset? Hashem is in control.'"

Oh, and if you're worried about what Henny's husband wore to shul that Succos, don't be. Henny found the dry cleaner's home number. She called him and after explaining the situation, he brought the suits to the Machlis home!

Henny taught in a seminary and would often talk to her students about how to control their anger. Here's how one student applied that life lesson:

The forgotten tefillin

Henny had a student whose son was going to put on tefillin for the very first time. That's always a special occasion, but this was extra-special, since the bar mitzvah boy had special needs. It had taken time, patience and perseverance to get him to learn how to put on his tefillin properly.

The big day arrived. The whole family got in the car to go to the Kosel where Henny's student's son would put tefillin on for the first time. After a half-hour's drive they could already see the Old City walls.

It was then that the boy's father said to his son, "Get your tefillin ready. We're almost there."

To everyone's surprise the boy answered, "I can't."

"Why not?"

"I forgot my tefillin at home."

You could feel the temperature in the car rising as the parents were about to explode with frustration and disappointment. Then the boy's mother remembered what she had learned from Henny about anger.

She took a deep breath and told her son, "It's O.K. I guess Hashem just doesn't want you to have your tefillin now."

The temperature in the car dropped and everyone accepted the situation. After all, it was what Hashem had wanted!

Pesach cleaning with Henny

We all clean for Pesach, but Henny took Pesach house-cleaning to a whole new level! She didn't just scrub the floors and clean out the closets, she used Pesach cleaning for "soul cleaning." There's *chametz* under the beds and *chametz* inside our hearts, she would say; bad *middos* that we would like to get rid of. Take that spray cleaner and wipe away laziness, jealousy, anger and *lashon hara*! Henny even advised people to make a list of bad character traits they want to get rid of before they start Pesach cleaning and to throw the list away on *erev Pesach*, into the fire where the *chametz* is being burned!

Henny's Recipes for Life

Henny taught that the word "Pesach" literally means "the mouth speaks" (*peh* — mouth, *sach* — speaks). We want Pesach to arrive after our mouths have spoken good things. The challenge of cleaning for Pesach is to avoid hurting anyone with our speech. Not to get angry at siblings, not to yell at them for not doing the Pesach cleaning the way you wanted them to, not to get upset with your parents when they ask you to clean out one more drawer.

Look at the *shemurah* matzah we will eat Seder night. It has been watched for months before Pesach so carefully not to become *chametz*. In the same way, we have to watch our mouths. We have to use our gift of speaking to give encouragement and positive reinforcement, not to angrily push people away or put them down.

Henny loved Torah learning. When she met people in the street she wouldn't just schmooze. It always came down to talking about Torah.

The "toys" Henny loved

Written in one of Henny's notebooks, in large Hebrew script, is a quote from Tehillim 119:92 : *Lulei Sorascha sha'ashu'ai az avaditi v'anyi.* Under the quote appears her English translation: "If Your Torah is not my exciting plaything, I will die." She translated *sha'ashu'ai as* "exciting plaything." For Henny, Torah study was something exciting, something she loved like a kid who loves toys.

Some people value money, Henny valued Torah. Not just in theory, but in action!

Forty shekels' worth of Torah

Henny would drive her second grader, Eliyahu, to school. But on Fridays she was too busy preparing for Shabbos to drive anyone anywhere, so she would send Eliyahu to school in a taxi. The trip cost forty shekels (which is more than $10.00, quite a bit to spend for a ride). Henny would send him even on the Fridays when he had overslept and was late for school. Though school got out early on Fridays and he would be in school for only an hour, she sent him.

Once, Eliyahu told his rebbi that he had come in a taxi for forty shekels. The rebbi said, "Forty shekels? You could buy a kugel for forty shekels." When Eliyahu came home he told his mother what his rebbi had said. She answered, "An hour of Torah is worth much more than a kugel."

CHAPTER 10

Calm, Calm, Calm

One of Henny's most striking traits was her ability to stay calm in any situation. Late at night, early in the morning— calm. Fifty guests waiting outside to come in for a meal and all the seats in the house are already filled with guests— calm. Shabbos is coming and the food hasn't been cooked? Absolutely calm.

Where does calmness of this sort come from? From stopping to believe that you control your life. True you can, and you should, make plans, but if those plans don't work out, or if reality suddenly doesn't work out like you hoped it would — maybe you didn't get into the bunk you were desperate to join, or you didn't get accepted to the school your friends are always going to, or it rained on the day of your major trip — realize that you have to give up control and let Hashem be your Guide. Let Him handle it His way.

You want to be calm, happy, satisfied? Learn the skill of surrendering to Hashem. Realize, as Henny used to say: "I'm not in charge, He is."

Henny's Recipes for Life

"The more I have *emunah*, the more chilled I am and I'm happier, because I know Hashem is running the world."

You know how when people travel, they often seem to get really nervous? Not Henny. When she was dealing with luggage check-in, passport control, security checks — all the stuff that makes people anxious — she stayed absolutely calm. Why? Because in addition to her suitcases and passport, she carried her *emunah* with her when she traveled. And when you live your life with *emunah*, even the mighty airlines are powerless against you!

Luggage 1

Henny had been to the United States for a visit and now it was time to fly home. Until recently, the airline had allowed each passenger to bring two pieces of luggage. Several months before this trip, the airline had changed its policy. Passengers could take only one piece of luggage for free; more would cost the passenger a lot of money.

Henny had four pieces of luggage!

Henny's sister-in-law, who was taking her to the airport, warned her that she would never get all those suitcases on the plane. But her sister-in-law's warnings did not faze Henny. If Hashem wanted her to get that luggage onto the plane, she would! She walked into the airport with all four pieces of luggage.

When the airlines changed their luggage policy, they let anyone who had booked their tickets before the rule came into effect take two pieces of luggage. Henny looked around at the check-in counter for religious girls who were traveling with only one piece of luggage. She found two girls who had booked their tickets before the luggage-policy change. They were each happy to check in a suitcase on their ticket. Two suitcases taken care of!

Now Henny had two suitcases still left, and no one to take her extra piece.

Henny approached the check-in counter. The lady at the counter checked her reservation on the computer. She smiled and said, "Because you booked your ticket months ago, before the rules changed, you are entitled to check in two suitcases."

Which just proves that even a top-of-the-line computer system was no match for Henny's *emunah*, because Henny had booked her ticket just three days before her trip, way after the one-suitcase rule had gone into effect!

Luggage 2

Henny had gone to New York for her mother's 80th birthday. With such a large family anxiously awaiting her at home, bringing presents back for all the children meant a lot of shopping for toys, candies, clothing and more.

When it was time to fly back to Eretz Yisrael, Henny's niece helped her pack. Each passenger was allowed only 50 pounds of luggage, and for an extra charge, 70 pounds. But that was the limit. Henny finished stuffing her duffel bag with all the goodies she was bringing back to the kids. Her niece picked up the duffel bag and said, "Aunt Henny, this for sure weighs more than 70 pounds."

"It's fine, it's fine." Henny suddenly remembered a family member who loved licorice. She opened the duffel bag and squeezed in yet another two-pound package of licorice. Then, with her niece's help, they schlepped the duffel bag onto a scale to weigh it. The scale read a whopping NINETY POUNDS!

"They will never let this go through baggage check," her niece warned her. "It's way over the seventy-pound limit." But of course, Henny knew that it was Hashem Who would decide how much she could take, and not an airline clerk.

At the airport, Henny calmly waited in line for check-in. When her turn came, the attendant at the check-in counter was fiddling with the scale. She looked up and said to Henny, "I'm sorry. The scale just broke. I'll check you in and then you can just put your suitcase over there with the other suitcases."

When Henny's niece heard how her aunt's luggage had made it through she remarked, "Aunt Henny's reality was that Hashem is in control and whatever He wants will happen, and she just has to talk to Him. It doesn't matter what the suitcase weighs, it doesn't matter the weight allowance. It just matters what Hashem wants."

When Henny's daughter Yael got married, Henny was already very sick. At one of the *sheva berachos*, Henny spoke. This is what she said:

Hashem's plan

"With all my kids, I expected that I would be the one to choose the best possible shidduch for them. I would be there for them, helping shop for their new home, arranging the wedding and the *sheva berachos*. Hashem looked at me and laughed. I got sick. So Yael's shidduch happened without me being involved. The wedding happened without my being involved. The *sheva berachos* happened without my lifting a finger to cook or prepare. Hashem has a plan and it's going to happen just the way He wants it. And the sooner we learn that, the happier we'll be."

One of the guests who often came to the Machlis home remembers that whether it was Shabbos, Yom Tov or Purim, Henny always radiated *yishuv hadaas*, tranquility.

Spilled wine

One Purim, he noticed the pools of spilled red wine on the table and more puddles of wine on the floor. Though he was used to Henny's calm and happy personality, today, he thought, things had really gotten out of control.

"I got nervous that it was too much of a mess even for Rebbetzin Machlis. I went over to offer to help clean up. I was just about to open my mouth when I took one look at her face and changed my mind. She was watching the merry antics of her guests with a big grin on her face. I knew that in her mind everything was just the way it was supposed to be. No need to clean up."

The guests settled down, it got quiet. All eyes were focused on Rabbi Machlis, who was about to make Kiddush. It was then that Yehoshua Machlis, sitting on his father's lap, decided to pick up the kiddush cup and see what his father's suit would look like if he poured the cup of wine on it. What a mess, what an embarrassing moment.

And more spilled wine

But neither Rabbi Machlis nor Henny reacted with anger or harsh words. Henny remained calm and patiently helped her husband clean up.

Rabbi Couzens, who was one of the guests present when this happened, asked Henny how she had stayed so calm. She told him, "When he grows up he won't spill wine on his father's suit. So why scold him?"

Henny's Recipes for Life

The Gemara teaches, "Any house where wine is not spilled like water has no blessing." Usually this is explained to mean that the house will be blessed with so much wine, it will be as cheap as water. But Henny had a different explanation.

When water spills, so what? You let it dry up, that's all. But when wine spills, *oy vey*, what a mess! And getting out all those wine stains means a trip to the cleaners. The Gemara means that any house where they don't treat spilled wine the way they would treat spilled water, THEN there's no blessing on that house. You have to be as calm when wine spills as you are when water spills, in order to be deserving of *berachah*.

CHAPTER 11
"It's Not Me."

Henny developed a strong sense of "It's not me." She looked at her accomplishments — feeding so many guests, making so many people Torah-observant, raising fourteen children — and she didn't feel that she did it. She knew she'd accomplished a lot, but she also knew that it was always Hashem making it happen. She thought of herself as a musician who knows she plays a violin really well, but in the end it's a God-given talent. This kind of thinking enabled her to not lash out at others when she was wrongly accused or insulted. Her "I" was not a capital "I," it was lower case "i." To put it another way, Henny was humble.

She would tell herself (and others whom she taught): "I have to know that me? I'm nothing. He's all there is. I shouldn't say, 'I do *chesed* and I have children and I am smart and I teach.' No! Hashem teaches and He has children and He does everything else."

The index finger

Henny had a friend who was forty years old. She was attractive, intelligent, and very put together, but with all her accomplishments and efforts, she had not found a shidduch and was still single.

She decided to go to a renowned *tzaddik* and ask for a *berachah*. The woman couldn't speak Hebrew so Henny went along with her to translate. Sitting together at the *tzaddik's* home, Henny explained the woman's situation and asked the *tzaddik* to give her a blessing that she should find a shidduch. The *tzaddik* showed them his index finger and moved it up and down.

Henny was puzzled. This was a *berachah*? Mystified, Henny asked the *tzaddik* to explain. While the *tzaddik* moved his finger up and down again, he said, "When your friend knows that she can't even do this without Hashem's help, then she'll find her *zivug*."

You know how people sometimes get really angry at someone? And how they occasionally lose it completely and start to yell?

Whose problem is it?

This unpleasant kind of encounter sometimes happened to Henny also. But her attitude toward being screamed at by someone who was furious was very creative. She would say, "Whose problem is this, mine or theirs?"

If it was clear that she hadn't done anything to deserve the person's anger, she would say to herself, "If she is criticizing me or even yelling at me, it's because she is missing something in her life. So I need to daven for her, 'Hashem, make her happy, because if she's screaming, she's clearly not happy. Happy people may get upset but they wouldn't scream. People who scream are usually under some kind of pressure, having nothing to do with whatever is upsetting them right now.'"

And if she thought the criticism was valid, she would say, "If it's my problem, and that's why the person got angry at me, then I'll work on it."

A good example of this happened once when Henny's son Eliyahu went with his mother to the Kosel. Henny would often go to the Kosel early in the morning to daven. It's not easy to find parking near the Kosel, so she would park in a space reserved for Kosel workers, who she knew did not arrive until seven in the morning. She always left before seven to free up the parking spot for the workers. But on the day Eliyahu was with her she took a little longer davening at the Kosel than she should have. She got back to her car at 7:05.

The worker whose parking space Henny had taken was waiting for her. He started screaming at her, "What's the matter with you!? How could you keep me waiting? You're selfish!" He went on and on, yelling at Henny for several minutes.

All through his tirade Henny just stood there and listened. She didn't try to defend herself, she didn't answer back. She just stood quietly listening to the man insult her. When he finally finished she apologized for being late and drove off.

Eliyahu was furious at how his mother had been treated. As they drove home he asked her, "Why didn't you defend yourself? After all, it was only five minutes."

She told Eliyahu, "It's not him; it's Him. It's not that man; it's Hashem. Maybe I have to fix what he's talking about, that I'm not on time to places. It has nothing to do with him. I really should have been back by 7 o' clock."

What a fantastic attitude in dealing with people who insult you!

Henny's Recipes for Life

If someone insults you, you are in pain. But what do you do with that pain? Do you strike back at that person, or do you run to Hashem? Hashem is the only Force that can give or take. Insults or flattery, He is the Source of all.

Henny used to tell her students about the time she was accused of being a thief:

Thief!

When Rabbi Nivin [one of the rabbis that Henny learned from] was very sick, I asked Hashem, "What do You want me to do for his *refuah*?" So the answer that popped into my head was: "Be quiet." Which meant that when people are *chutzpadik*, angry or insulting, I shouldn't give them any power over me by arguing with them. Instead I should be quiet, submissive and know that it's coming from HaKadosh Baruch Hu.

My chance to practice this wasn't long in coming. One morning one of the people who come to the house said, "I had $10.00 in my pocketbook and you stole it on Shabbos." I thought: *How absurd! I did no such thing.* Now you have to understand, this person was not so normal. She said, "You're a thief! You're a *ganav*!"

I wanted to answer, "No, it couldn't have been me. I don't even touch money on Shabbos." But I didn't say that. I remembered to be quiet. Not a quietness of weakness, but a quietness of strength. I thought, *What does Hashem want?* So right away I thought, *Oh, Hashem wants me not to be a ganav.* I began to think. How am I a *ganav*?

Then I realized that on Shabbos I had a lot of guests, and a lot of people came up to me and gave me compliments, "Oh, what you do in your house is so great! It's so wonderful!" So I don't always remember to say to Hashem, "Really it's Your compliment." So in a way I'm a *ganav*. I steal Hashem's compliments, His honor. I take it for myself, thinking like, "It's great how **we** do *kiruv*." So Hashem wanted me to know, "Don't be a *ganav*. Don't steal for yourself what belongs to Me."

As soon as I finished figuring out that I am a thief, you will never guess what happened! My accuser said, "Oh, I guess you didn't touch the money," and she left my house.

The Gemara says that a person who is hurt or insulted and doesn't answer back is as strong as the sun and will find their name on the Almighty's list of "lovers of Hashem." If we could take a peek at that list for sure we would see Henny's name on it, and probably in big letters.

First-day-of-school jitters

Tova was a young mother trying to prepare her children for the first day of school. She was jittery, her kids were even more jittery. There was so much to do! Choosing the right clothes, putting together everyone's books and pencil cases, organizing the lunches, snacks and backpacks. Everyone was tense, nervous and excited.

The doorbell rang. Tova dropped what she was doing and ran to answer it.

There was no one there.

The family went back to their school preps. Again, the doorbell rang. Again, no one there. But this time Tova could see the figures of children running away, laughing. And she recognized those kids.

Grumbling, she turned back to what she was doing. And suddenly the bell rang once again.

Tova lost it. Hardly thinking, she raced over the Machlis home. Henny greeted her with a smile, but there was no smile in return.

"I'm in middle of preparing my kids for school and your kids are playing pranks! Can't you control your children!!!?? Keep them away from my door!"

Henny apologized, promising to keep a closer watch on her children. Tova stomped away, still upset, when she heard Henny's voice calling to her. "You should see *nachas* from your kids this year, they should all do well in school."

Tova remembers her reaction. "I had been mean and nasty to her and she was blessing me and my kids? Wow!"

The misunderstanding

You may be saying to yourself, "Look, bottom line it was her kids who caused the trouble so she should apologize. And she came late, even if it was only five minutes so, again, it's right for her to say she's sorry. But what would happen if someone accused Henny of doing something wrong, and she had never done it? When someone else's mistake got her into trouble? What would she do then?"

Actually, something like that did happen to Henny, and she passed her test with flying colors. We even know what she said, because it was recorded.

This is what happened:

One of Rebbetzin Henny's seminary students called her mother in America. After the usual, "Hi, how are you?" she told her mother what she had learned in Henny's class.

"Ma, remember I told you we have a teacher Rebbetzin Machlis who's famous for having an open house every Shabbos with a hundred guests? Well, today she taught us awesome stuff. All about *hisbodedus* and it's so important that if we don't do it for an hour a day we're not Jewish."

Needless to say, the mother was pretty shocked to hear her daughter talking that way. After she finished talking with her daughter she immediately called the head of the seminary and angrily complained. "What kind of nonsense are you teaching there?" The school head got an earful from the mother and a full report on what Rebbetzin Machlis had supposedly taught.

The next time Henny came to teach, the school head met her at the door of her office with a grim look on her face and asked if she could step into her office for a minute. Henny said later that it reminded her of being called into the principal's office when she was a little girl. They sat down and the school head asked Henny to explain how she could teach the students that if someone doesn't do *hisbodedus* they are not Jewish, and that *hisbodedus* should be done for an hour a day? Henny was shocked. "I never said such a thing! I told the girls to try *hisbodedus* for FIVE MINUTES A DAY, that all." The school head then asked Henny to go to her class and set them straight on what she had said.

Quite an embarrassing experience, right? Many people would walk into the classroom with some sharp and sarcastic words for the students, asking them to, "Please listen ***carefully*** this time!" or "Girls, why don't you pay attention instead of texting? You got me in trouble with the administration."

But not Rebbetzin Henny. This is an accurate transcript of what she told the class:

"Now I just spoke with Mrs. __________ and she said that there was a miscommunication about something I'm trying to teach and something you understood. So she said that one mother called her up and said that her daughter said that Rebbetzin Machlis said if you don't do an hour of *hisbodedus* a day, you're not a Jew. And she said that many other girls had the misconception that I said that you must do an hour a day of *hisbodedus*. So I'll just clarify. First of all, we'll clarify what the homework is. The homework is to do five minutes of *hisbodedus* a day, to try to use the first two minutes to thank Hashem for anything and everything. Try to do a half a minute to a minute of praise. "

No reprimand or words of disapproval. No mentioning the name of the student who'd gotten it so wrong. It was a mistake, that's all. Though the mistake caused the Rebbetzin to be blamed for something she didn't do, she spoke to the girls in a tone of voice that was warm and patient. She set the record straight without causing the girls any embarrassment or making them feel that she disapproved of them in any way.

That's how you speak when you see yourself as a "lower case i."

Bouncing checks

In Eretz Yisrael, when someone wants immediate cash in shekels for foreign currency checks they often go to a moneychanger. The moneychanger is taking a risk, because the checks he was given may bounce. That means that whoever wrote the check didn't have enough money in the bank to cover it — and the check is worthless. But the moneychanger already gave his cash away! When a moneychanger gets a check like that, he usually gets very angry. Often he can be very unpleasant about it, screaming and threatening and demanding his money back immediately.

The Machlises had a moneychanger they worked with frequently. People from countries outside of Israel sometimes gave them checks as contributions, to help out with the costs of hosting so many people. The Machlises would go to this moneychanger to turn the checks into shekels, which they'd use to buy the food. Every so often the checks would bounce and the moneychanger would call, screaming at Henny and asking for his money back.

When Henny passed away this is what the moneychanger said to her son, Moshe Machlis, when he was sitting *shivah* for his mom:

"I was so rude to her when I called her about bad checks. But unlike my other customers who made excuses, she was never defensive. She never said it wasn't her fault, even though the truth was she didn't give me a bad check on purpose. How could she know that a check she was sent was bad? She only wanted me to feel better. She always said, 'I understand you. You're right.' Now that she is gone I feel so bad. Your mother treated me so well, though I was rude to her. I am so ashamed and sorry for the way I behaved. When you visit your mother's grave please, please beg her to forgive me."

CHAPTER 12
The Price of Peace

Hey, we all like peace, right? We all agree that it's better to have *shalom* than to fight.

But what if the price of keeping peace means giving up something that belongs to you, or that you really want to do? Would you do that? Would you sacrifice what you want — and even what you deserve — for the sake of peace?

If you do, you'd be called a *vatran*. That's the word for someone who gives things up, even if rightfully theirs, for the sake of peace.

Someone like Henny Machlis.

A young couple was moving into a new apartment and didn't want to pay for a moving van. Instead, they borrowed the Machlises' van.

The van

"We just need it for moving day," they assured Henny.

Moving day came and went. And another day passed, and another. Still the couple hadn't returned the van. Finally they returned it, over a week later!

Bad enough that they'd returned it late but even worse, the van was damaged from the furniture and heavy appliances they had transported inside it. Henny pointed it out, and politely asked them to repair the damage. Not only didn't they apologize for not bringing the van back when they had promised, but they were very cool about the damage. "It isn't so bad," they said. "What's the big deal?"

Henny tried to get them to change their minds and take responsibility to pay for the damage they'd caused. It didn't help. She realized that if she pushed any more it would just cause a fight, a *machlokes*, so she decided to just drop it and leave the couple alone. She told herself, "It's from Hashem."

Not long after her decision to avoid a fight, one of her daughters, who had been very sick, had a full and unexpected recovery.

Henny said, "Thank You, Hashem, that You took the car. The car is dead, and my daughter is alive."

The broken leg

Imagine what your parents would do if your day camp called them and told them that they are really very sorry to give them the news that you're in a cast, because a counselor had jumped on you and accidentally broken your leg.

Your parents would be really upset and angry at the camp and the counselor. They would probably want to sue the camp because of your injury.

This actually happened to Batsheva Machlis. Do you know what her parents did? Even though all their friends advised them to sue the camp, for the sake of *shalom* they were *mevater* their rights and decided not to sue.

But the story doesn't end there.

Thinking about what had happened, Henny realized that the counselor must be feeling very guilty, so she called the girl up and reassured her. "Don't worry. It could happen to anyone. Don't feel bad."

Batsheva, and all the Machlis children, learned the lessons of being *mevater* all through her life. Talking about her broken leg, she says: "My parents were always *mevater*. They would say, 'Let it go. It doesn't matter.' They always taught us to be *mevater*. And not just outwardly. They taught us to never keep a grudge in our heart."

No!

On the one hand, it's great to give in for the sake of peace. On the other hand, there are times when you have to know your boundaries. There are times when you do have to stand up and say, "NO!"

Henny was such a giving person, it was hard for her to learn to say "No." But as she got older, she told people that she realized that it was a mitzvah for her to take care of herself, as well as taking care of the rest of Klal Yisrael! She once told someone: "I realize that it's Hashem's will that I take care of my physical, emotional and psychological needs."

CHAPTER 13

Talk to Hashem!

Henny didn't just talk to Hashem three times a day, at Shacharis, Minchah and Maariv. She spoke to Him a hundred times a day: asking, praying, hoping and thanking. She would ask to be close to Him. She would pray for the Jewish people after a terror attack, or for someone who was sick. She would share her hopes that she could find the money for braces for her kids or just the right outfit for Yom Tov. She would thank Him when a child's fever went down or her car started even though she'd forgotten to turn off the lights. There was nothing that was out of His power to help her with, and nothing too small or insignificant to ask for.

Henny loved to tell over this story about the power of prayer:

Rav Elyashiv's answer

It happened fifteen years ago, when a wave of Palestinian terror, called the "intifada," was raging. Terrorists were blowing themselves — and innocent civilians — up on buses and in the streets. Every week there were stories of more tragedies, more people murdered. The situation was deadly and frightening for the Jews in Eretz Yisrael.

Rebbetzin Tziporah Heller, a well-known teacher in Yerushalayim and a friend of Henny's, went to Rav Elyashiv *zt"l* for advice. "What should I do to help?" she asked the Rav. "Should I go to rallies? Should I write letters? Is there anything to do? Or *rak l'hispallel* — just daven?"

"RAK l'hispallel? JUST daven?" Rav Elyashiv answered. *"Zeh kol mah she'yeish! Zeh hakol*! That's all there is! Davening is everything!"

The last summer of her life, Henny asked a rabbi to give over this message on her behalf to his students:

"Please tell everyone this. As much as it's important to go to holy places and to speak to holy people, everyone has to know that we should talk to Hashem. We should just turn to Hashem, we have a direct line!"

The Gulf War

The year was 1991. The Gulf War had begun. America and its allies were fighting against Saddam Hussein, the evil, murderous dictator of Iraq. He had threatened to bomb Israel if America attacked.

It was known that Saddam had chemical weapons. There was a real expectation that besides conventional bombs (which are bad enough!) Saddam would hit Israel with missiles tipped with poison gas.

In the months before the war the population of Eretz Yisrael prepared themselves for the worst. All the citizens, even children, were given gas masks. Everyone was instructed to prepare one "sealed room" in their homes. That was a room where the windows were covered with plastic, closing the room off so poison gas couldn't seep in. The people were told that if they heard warning sirens signaling an incoming attack, they should run to the nearest sealed rooms and put on their gas masks, and then wait for the all-clear signal before leaving the sealed room.

One Friday night, right at the beginning of the war, the sirens went off, WOOOOOOOOH! WOOOOOOH! Fear and panic gripped families. Everyone sprang into action, grabbing their children, entering the sealed rooms and putting on gas masks.

Sitting in their sealed rooms, everyone prayed. They prayed it shouldn't be a gas attack, prayed that the missile would fall somewhere in a field and not hurt anyone. Most everyone who lived through it would never forget that Friday-night attack. Imagine: One moment a family is at the Shabbos table singing *Shalom Aleichem*; the next, they're huddled in a stuffy room, wearing uncomfortable gas masks, wondering where the missile will fall.

When Henny looked back on that Friday night she remembered the fear. She remembered what it was like seeing her precious children in gas masks. But she also remembered the intensity of the prayers she said for the safety of all the Jews in Israel, and the realization that in this special moment all of the Jews of Eretz Yisrael were praying together. Even when the all clear was sounded, instead of breathing a sigh of relief that they weren't hit and bursting out of their sealed room, Henny just stayed on, her eyes closed, as she davened for the safety of the people who might have been hurt by the missile attack.

At Henny's *shivah* a woman had this story to tell:

***Geulah*!**

"I was praying at the Kotel when I heard uncontrollable, intense weeping and sobbing. A woman was leaning against the Wall, begging for the *geulah*. I looked up and next to me was standing your mother."

Henny's Recipes for Life

Henny taught that we shouldn't be sad or discouraged. There's only prayer and we shouldn't be lazy about it.

Henny would tell over the story about a couple from a small village who traveled to the Baal Shem Tov to get a *berachah* to have a baby. And he said, "No, I'm not giving you a *berachah*." They went back again to get a *berachah* for a baby. But the Baal Shem still wouldn't give them the *berachah*.

When they returned home and told their parents what happened, their parents said, "Don't come back here till you have a *berachah* to have a baby."

So they went back to Mezhibozh to the Baal Shem Tov. Again they met with the Baal Shem Tov. We must have a *berachah* for a baby or we can't go home," they told him.

He said, "You are not getting a *berachah* from me.'"

They went back to the inn where they were staying and in the privacy of their small room they cried and cried. They asked Hashem to have mercy on them and send them a baby.

And not long afterward, their heartfelt prayers were answered, and they held a beautiful newborn in their arms.

When the baby was a little older, they returned to the Baal Shem Tov and asked, "Why didn't you give us a *berachah*?"

So he said, "You wanted me to do the work, but Hashem wanted you to do the work."

When we need help, don't be lazy, ask Him. It could be for anything. Help me pass my driving test, help me not to fight with my parents, help me find a perfect dress for Pesach. Whatever we want to get done, we need help. We need help but *we* have to do the work — with sincere prayer!

Lost!

The Machlis family was in a panic. Their baby sister Yael was missing! They looked in the playground, searched the house. No Yael. The family started to knock on neighbors' doors. "Did anyone see Yael? Is she here?" Desperate, the family called Hatzalah and the police to report a missing child.

While the family was doing everything they could, Henny did what she did best. She stayed in her husband's study davening, crying over Tehillim, begging that her daughter be found.

And, yes, little Yael was finally discovered, sleeping happily under a blanket where no one noticed her. *Baruch Hashem*!

Henny's Recipes for Life

What does the Gemara mean when it teaches that "ten parts of speech" were given to the world, and women have nine of them? According to Henny, it means that women were given an extraordinary amount of speech: to use for davening and to teach the world the importance of prayer.

Emergency-room prayers

Mazel tov! Henny's daughter Elisheva had a baby.

But — *uh oh*. Not long after her son's bris she began to feel very sick. Elisheva's husband and her mother Henny were concerned, and they brought her to the emergency room.

Since it was so soon after childbirth, the doctors ran a lot of tests, but they didn't find anything. "Go home and rest," they recommended, "you'll be fine."

Which goes to show that doctors don't always know everything, because as they handed Elisheva her discharge papers, she fell down, unconscious!

The doctors came running and began to try and revive her.

And Henny? She did what she did best; she stood over her daughter and began to pray. The prayers of a mother for her child, lying unconscious, surrounded by doctors who are having a hard time bringing her back.

Ignoring everything going on around her, Henny poured her heart out: "Hashem, You have to bring my daughter back. She has a little baby. He's nine days old. There's no way that You can't bring her back. Hashem, *b'zechus* Sarah Imeinu and *b'zechus* Avraham Avinu, Yitzchak Avinu, Yaakov Avinu, bring my daughter back. *B'zechus* Dovid HaMelech, *b'zechus* Rabbi Shimon bar Yochai, *b'zechus* Reb Usher, *b'zechus* all of the *tzaddikim*, please bring my daughter back."

Henny's voice was raised in prayer and nurses don't like that kind of commotion. They asked her to leave but Henny, completely involved in her *tefillos*, ignored them.

Finally, a nurse threatened to call Security.

It was only then that Henny gave them her attention. "You can call Security, you can call the police. I'm staying here and I'm not leaving."

And, as Elisheva finishes the story: "It was then that I opened my eyes. My mom's prayers brought me back."

Besides talking to Hashem constantly, Henny also davened three times a day: Shacharis, Minchah and Maariv. Even though women don't have the same obligation to pray three times a day, like men do, she was careful to do so anyway, even when it was hard — and sometimes when it seemed almost impossible.

3X Daily

Cancer treatments are tough on the body. When Henny went for her therapy she always thought ahead, and davened before her treatment began, in case she would be too weak to do so afterward. At the end of her life, though she was so sick and weak, she would not go to sleep without having davened Maariv first.

Window to greatness

Henny was certainly busier than your average person. She had fourteen kids. That keeps a person pretty busy. She had an open house, and shopped, cooked and cleaned up after more than a hundred people every Shabbos. That keeps a person even busier! And during the week, she taught in seminaries, went to *shiurim* and did tons of *chesed*.

And yet, with all that, she managed to find time for davening. Here is what she once told her seminary students about her *tefillah* schedule. It's a peek into Henny's davening life, a window to greatness.

This is how the class discussion went:

Rebbetzin Machlis: I daven three *tefillos* a day including the *Korbanos*. I skip nothing. I try to have *kavannah* for every word I say. I'm just sharing that with you.

Student: You have time to daven every day?

Rebbetzin Machlis: I make time.

Student: Three *tefillos* plus an hour of *hisbodedus*?

Rebbetzin Machlis: I try, yes. I try. I ask HaKadosh Baruch Hu even for that. I try to say a lot of Tehillim on Shabbos, but I had a lot of my married children over this Shabbos, and in addition a special couple that needed a lot of guidance, so I wasn't able to finish Tehillim. To make up for what I missed on Shabbos, today I woke up at 4 a.m., an hour and a half earlier than usual, to finish my Tehillim.

Henny's grandson Asher Storch remembers how his Savta davened: "She prayed calmly, without rushing. Let's say she was late to go somewhere; it didn't matter, she didn't rush davening. Other people if they are late for an appointment would rush through their davening. But not Savta."

Henny's Recipes for Life

Do you want the *geulah* to come? You want to see Mashiach? Then work to perfect your *ahavas Yisrael*, your love for your fellow Jews. That's the Amshinover Rebbe's advice.

One part of *ahavas Yisrael* is not to have negative thoughts about others. That may be easy with the person you pass in the street, and a bit harder with the kids in your class. But with family, like your infuriating younger sibling or the older sister who bosses everyone around, having *ahavas Yisrael* for them can be very hard! Can anything be done about that?

Henny's answer is: Yes! Pray. Ask Hashem for help.

Henny sometimes also found *ahavas Yisrael* for her family a challenge. She would daven, "Hashem, Hashem, help me see the good. You want me to see the good in them and we want You to see the good in us. Help me!"

Something Henny learned from Rav Usher helped her as well. Rav Usher wrote that people like to fantasize. "My life would be a lot better if only—I had been born to a different family— I lived somewhere else— my family had more money— THEN my life would be perfect, I would be happy. This kind of thinking IS A LIE. Hashem gave us the most amazing life, the exact life we should be leading. Hashem wants us to be in this family, with these brothers and sisters, and in this house. He wants us to LOVE it and to know it's all *CHESED* from Him.

When it comes to everyone, and especially our own family, the Almighty wants us to wear "positive glasses" and to see the good in what He gives us. Not to complain about what we don't have, but to appreciate what we do have.

And, like Henny, we should pray, "Hashem, just like You want me to see the positive in my family and neighbors, please, look down and see the positive in Am Yisrael. And bring the complete redemption now."

Henny's prayer lifestyle made an impression on others and especially on her children. Her daughter Tamar confesses that sometimes

Too late

by the time her day ends, she feels it's just too late and she is too tired to daven Maariv. But then she tells herself, "Ima would daven Maariv, no matter how tired she was, no matter how sick she was." With her mother as a model Tamar doesn't go to sleep without having davened Maariv.

Henny's Recipes for Life

Communicating with the Almighty, having a relationship with Him, requires prayer. But women and girls sometimes don't have time to say the formal prayers. They are busy taking care of their children or babysitting for their siblings. Then they just have to talk to Hashem.

You're trying to have a relationship with HaKadosh Baruch Hu, and you do that through prayer. But it depends on the circumstances. If a person is so busy, they just had a baby, or whatever it is, they have to learn to talk to HaKadosh Baruch Hu.

There is always time to say, "I love You," or "I want to love You," or "Help me love You." And every time you do that you're fulfilling the *mitzvas asei d'Oraisa* of "*V'ahavta es Hashem Elokecha,* Love the Lord your God."

CHAPTER 14

Tehillim Power

Henny communicated with Hashem in many ways: through her *hisbodedus*, her three daily *tefillos*, her constant speaking to Him and, especially, through reciting Tehillim.

She said Tehillim for all kinds of situations: to help her kids when they were struggling in school or at home, on behalf of others who needed God's help or for herself when she was facing a challenge.

She would say Tehillim at home and at Shmuel HaNavi's *kever* or the Kosel. She would also visit the *kever* of Shimon HaTzaddik, a fifteen-minute walk from her home, and say her Tehillim there. When there was an emergency — a marriage that was breaking up, a Jew about to intermarry, someone suffering from a terrible disease or wounded in a horrific accident — she would say the ENTIRE FIVE BOOKS OF TEHILLIM in one go.

Henny "talking" to Hashem

It was absolutely astonishing what Henny's Tehillim could accomplish.

Once, a friend of Henny's was waiting for her baby to be born. It was

Henny, the master teacher

past the time that the doctors had said it would happen and she was feeling upset and anxious. Henny, who knew about her friend's situation, decided to say all of Tehillim. One chapter, another chapter, and another — she was up until six in the morning, tearfully begging for Hashem's help. She didn't finish until six in the morning. Soon after she got the happy news: her friend had a healthy baby at six in the morning! How's that for timing?

Here are some more fascinating examples of Henny's Tehillim power.

The divorce

During her last year of life, Henny's son Yehoshua decided to give his mother a gift. Since she loved music, he organized a small concert for her at a friend's apartment. Moshe Rosenthal, Henny's son-in-law, was one of the guests. Henny was enjoying the concert when she noticed someone pouring his heart out to Moshe.

After the concert Henny told Moshe, "The fellow you were talking with, I see he's in pain. What's going on? Can we help?"

Moshe told Henny all about his friend, Chezky, and his problem. Chezky's *shalom bayis* had gotten so bad that his wife wanted to divorce him. But he wanted to stay married! He still loved his wife and they had seven children who would be devastated by the divorce. Chezky didn't want the family to break up and had tried and tried to convince his wife to stay married but she refused to listen to him.

Henny was already sick when she took this picture with Yehoshua

They had an appointment at the *beis din,* where he was finally going to give her a divorce. He was totally brokenhearted over losing his wife and breaking up his family.

"It's very sad," Moshe said. "And there's nothing we can do for him."

It was one in the morning, and Henny was weak and exhausted from her chemotherapy treatments, but after hearing the terrible story of a Jewish marriage with seven kids breaking up, Henny told her son and son-in-law, "There is something we can do to help. We've got to daven for him. Right now."

"Ma, its late," her son Yehoshua protested. "You're tired. Go to sleep, we can daven for him tomorrow."

"No, he's in terrible pain," Henny insisted. (And wasn't *she*?) "We have to daven for him right now. Get me a *sefer* Tehillim."

The three then sat down and said Tehillim for most of the night.

Want to know how the story ends?

Not long after that night of prayer, Chezky and his wife stood before the *beis din*. One of the judges began the proceedings by asking Chezky's wife, "Do you want *shalom bayis,* or do you want a divorce?"

Her answer astonished the *beis din* and Chezky. "I don't want a divorce," she said, turning to her shocked husband. "I want to stay married to you."

The *dayan*, the judge, later told Chezky that in 35 years of overseeing thousands of divorces, something like this had never ever happened before.

They left the *beis din*, the family stayed together and their *shalom bayis* got better and better, until eventually Chezky and his wife had a wonderful marriage. Chezky felt something miraculous had happened in his life, but as happy as he was he couldn't help but wonder how at the last minute his wife had changed her mind and decided to stay married.

He found his answer when he flew to Israel for Henny Machlis's *shivah* and heard from Moshe about Henny's davening for him that night. Then he understood. As Chezky said, "I have no doubt that it was her prayers that saved my marriage."

Henny's Recipes for Life

We shouldn't give up, not on our older single siblings, not on a sick relative and not on ourselves. We shouldn't give up.

We have to really believe that Hashem can help us. Have *emunah* and not give up, even when things look bad, even if it seems hopeless. I talk to so many people who tell me, "I daven, daven, daven, and nothing is moving." That is the Satan fooling you. The world is moving under us speeding through space. Do we feel it? No. Is it happening? Yes! When we pray, we are moving worlds. Don't give up just because you don't see results. And always talk to Hashem.

Often, Henny needed shekels for her *chesed* projects. Sometimes she needed small amounts, other times it was a lot of money. People would send Henny dollar checks to use for *tzedakah*. She would take those checks to a moneychanger, who would cash the checks and give her shekels to use.

Fifty thousand shekels

A moneychanger isn't like a bank. Sometimes he runs out of shekels. Once, Henny came in and asked for 50,000 shekels (which come out to more than $10,000). "I can't help you," he said. "We don't have that much on hand now. Come back tomorrow, maybe then I'll have it."

If that happened to you or me, we would probably just go home and try again the next day. Henny had a different approach. She sat in the moneychanger's store and said Tehillim. After a while a customer suddenly appeared bringing 50,000 shekels to change into dollars — shekels that could now be given to Henny, still sitting quietly looking into her Tehillim.

Pretty cute story, right? But what's more amazing, the moneychanger told Henny's son Moshe that it happened not just that once, but several times: Henny just sat and prayed until the money she needed was brought in by someone.

CHAPTER 15:

Saying Goodbye

Being sick is hard. It tests our faith in Hashem, and it hurts. It's even hard to read about. Yet when we see someone who turns illness into a means of deepening the connection to Hashem, the pain can become a source of inspiration to us.

If you are brave and can read this chapter of how Henny faced the illness that took her life, you will experience how a righteous woman dealt with suffering, how an already great woman's suffering brought her to incredible heights of *emunah* and *bitachon*. You will learn many important lessons about life, and you will be amazed and inspired by Henny's bravery and strength and acceptance of Hashem's will. (You may also cry a little; that's O.K.)

Henny become ill with cancer. One of the most difficult challenges for Henny when she became sick was that all the energy she had to cook for so many people, to pray late into the night, to raise fourteen kids — all of that energy was gone. Now instead of caring for others she had to rely on others to care for her.

Though Henny had very strong faith in Hashem even before she got struck by a horrible illness, it was still quite a battle for her to learn to accept this new and difficult reality. She fought, she asked questions, she davened and, as you will see, she finally won the last battle of her life.

Henny's Recipes for Life

Ever feel you're having a rough time? Someone in the family is sick, or it's your worst year in school ever? Here's something that may help. It's what Henny would tell people going through hard times.

Tell yourself, Hashem just wants me to remember that I'm not in charge. He is. Everything will be O.K. *because* He's in charge! Cheer up, Mashiach is coming very soon.

Fruit platters

Henny told her students, "I received the many fruit platters and letters and notes and emails that everybody sent, and I did have a few weeks in the course of this time that I was not able to move, literally. Forget about davening, forget about Tehillim; I wasn't able to do anything. But knowing that there were people who were davening for me and who were doing their special contribution in their *avodas Hashem* gave me a tremendous amount of inner strength and a tremendous amount of joy when I was really low and really weak and really troubled. And you were all a very tremendous source of strength for me."

At the last years of her life Henny reached an extremely high level of *emunah*. She recognized that only Hashem is in control. That was her last, most powerful message to us. She would tell others:

"I'm a baby in Hashem's baby carriage. I want to know how Hashem is going to cure me, and it looks like it's never going to happen. But I don't have to know. I'm giving up my mind to Him."

Henny learned: We don't have to understand everything Hashem does. We have to accept the Almighty's will. And we have to try and do that with love.

Henny's Recipes for Life

When Henny was in the hospital, sick and in excruciating pain, her son asked her, "Why do you tell people who come to visit that you feel fine?"

She answered, "Because I'm suffering, why do they have to suffer? Because I have pain, why do I have to give them pain?"

Henny's treatments to fight the cancer were very hard for her, physically and emotionally. So what do Jews do when they are in pain? They go to a rabbi, of course, for comfort, advice and a *berachah*.

Second-in-command

Once, Henny was weak, sad and totally overwhelmed by what she was going through. She went to discuss her feelings with Rav Avraham Harari, and she said to him, "Why is it so hard for me?"

He said, "You tell me. You know."

Henny said, "Come on, why is this chemo so hard for me? Like it's just really hard."

And he said, "Because you're not being *mekabel*; you're not accepting what Hashem wants for you."

She burst out crying and said, "You're absolutely right. I don't want this. I don't want chemo. I don't want to be sick. I don't want this whole package."

So he said, "But *Hu Echad v'ein sheni*. There's only one God and there is no second. Did He appoint you His second-in-command?"

Rav Harari's words comforted her and over time Henny made peace with her situation. She would say, "Hashem wants me to be closer to Him, that's why He's giving me this pain."

Before receiving her chemotherapy injections and treatments, she would always say, "Hashem, You're the doctor. You will make me feel better. You're going to make the treatment go well."

She would also say, "Hashem, thank You."

Her son Yehoshua once asked her, "What are you thanking Hashem for?"

His mom told him, "Thank You for everything You've given me. Thank You for the cancer. But I've had enough. Now please take it back."

Henny's Recipes for Life

In the Megillah it says that Esther tells Mordechai, "I'm not going to King Achashveirosh.'" And he says to her, "If you don't go, you and your father's house will be destroyed, and maybe this is the reason you were chosen to be queen." There are great Rabbanim who ask: What was Esther saying? She surely wasn't afraid to go to the king, because she lived in his palace and she was his queen. But what she meant was: "Why do I have to go to the king? I'll talk to Hashem. This Achashveirosh is nothing compared to Hashem. If I can deal directly with Hashem, the King of kings, why should I go to Achashveirosh? I don't have to go to him."

So Mordechai says, "Sorry, you have to do *hishtadlus*, to make an effort to actively do something to save the Jews. Go!" And she goes.

Henny explained, "Esther understood that Achashveirosh was nothing. Only Hashem has power in this world. So when I had to do chemo, I kept on saying I want to be cured with *emunah*, I want be cured with *emunah*. But Hashem kept saying, you have do chemo, you have to do chemo, you have to make efforts.

"I'm going to doctors and CTs and everything, but I say Hashem, help me have the *emunah* to know that it's all You. You're healing me. You'll do it any way You want; I don't care, pick and choose, whatever's good for You. Help me not interfere. So this is the prayer that I say: Hashem, help me anoint You King."

Henny was in pain and suffering very much, yet when the opportunity came she always put aside her own problems and listened and comforted others. For someone who is sick that is an enormous achievement of strength of will.

The volunteer

Chaya is a volunteer for the Lakewood's Bikur Cholim society. Once a week she drives cancer patients to Manhattan for treatment at Sloan-Kettering. She brings the patient to the hospital and waits with her throughout the treatment, offering help and moral support. One day, Chaya was sitting in the waiting room waiting for the woman she was with to finish her treatment. She met another religious Jewish woman and they started to chat. The other woman was upbeat and lively. She told Chaya stories, inspired her with *divrei Torah* and gave her *chizuk*.

After a while, Chaya said, "You're amazing. Who are you here with?"

"What do you mean?"

"I mean, who did you bring here for treatment?"

"Who did I bring? I'm the one who's here for treatment."

Chaya was totally blown away. The woman who has been inspiring her was herself a cancer patient, none other than Henny Machlis.

Henny was feeling sick but she has no choice, she had to go to Sloan-Kettering for her next round of chemo. A woman volunteered to drive Henny and her daughter from Brooklyn to the hospital in Manhattan.

The troubled driver

Henny got into the car and after some small talk Henny realized that the driver was going through a hard time. So the whole way to Manhattan, Henny encouraged the driver to talk about her problems. At the end of the ride, the driver says, "I'm so embarrassed. I gave you a ride, and you gave me what I needed the whole way here." When the car pulled away, Henny confided to her daughter, "I was in crazy pain the whole time."

After her mother passed away, Henny's daughter Sara told people that while Henny was going through the treatments, she would take three of her children with her. Why? She didn't need three people to help her.

Sick people, sick souls

She explained that Henny had asked herself, "Why is the Almighty sending me to spend so much time in the hospital? There must be a reason." After giving it much thought, she decided it was to pray for the sick people in the hospitals, and for the souls of the Jews in the hospital, sick or well, who were disconnected from Hashem and from His Torah.

She asked her children to come along and gave us each of them a job. "You pray for me," she said to one, "you pray for the sick to get better," she told the second, "and you pray that Hashem returns the lost souls back to *Yiddishkeit*," she told her third child.

That was a Henny Machlis lesson for a lifetime, a lesson in both the power of prayer and our responsibility to the people around us!

The Gemara says that you if you really want to know the true character of someone, see how they act when they are drunk or angry: *bi'kiso* (his pocket), *b'kaaso* (his anger) and *b'koso* (his drinking). That's when a person's true personality comes out. When angry or drunk, people say what they are honestly thinking. There is another time when that happens as well: when people are regaining consciousness after having been put to sleep with anesthesia for an operation or medical procedure. The first things patients say as they wake up from under anesthesia can tell you a lot about them.

Sing me a song

Henny's daughter Yocheved remembers the time when she was with her mom after surgery in the recovery room. When her mother started to wake up the first thing she said was, "I'm sorry I'm not talking to you."

Yocheved said, "Ima, why are you thinking about me? I'm here for you." But always, even when only partially awake, Henny was always thinking about others, in this case feeling bad she couldn't schmooze with her daughter.

And then Henny asked her daughter to sing "*Nishmas kol chai,*" a song that had had appeared on a CD put out by Yocheved's husband. It was a beautiful song about how every living being blesses and thanks Hashem.

The first thing that comes out of the mouths of many people when they wake up after surgery is, "Am I O.K.? Was the surgery successful?" Henny was just thinking about not hurting Yocheved's feelings and thanking Hashem. For her, it was always "not about me." It was about others — and about Him.

Two months before Henny died she was a very, very, sick woman. Even then, though her body was weakened by cancer, Henny managed to be happy and do the impossible.

Mind over body

Not long before her death, Henny spent Shabbos with her nephew, Rabbi Yisrael Stone, who lived on the sixth floor of a Manhattan apartment building.

On Friday night, Henny didn't feel well. The next morning Rabbi Stone left to shul, assuming his aunt would either daven at home or just rest, which made it all the more shocking when, during Shacharis, he looked up and noticed a woman walking in: his Aunt Henny!

Rabbi Stone remembers that moment vividly: "I was in shock! Not only did she come to shul but she had a happy look on her face. Later I found out that first she had gone to a shul near our house, but she came late and missed the Torah reading. So she said, 'I have to hear *krias haTorah.*' So she walked to my shul, Chabad, because she knew we start later. And she got there in time to hear the Torah reading."

It was a long walk back, but Henny somehow made it. When they finally came to Rabbi Stone's building, he suggested that his aunt use the Shabbos elevator, but Henny refused.

And this sick, weary, weak — and very determined — woman walked up all seventy steps, to his sixth-floor apartment.

The last month

Henny spent her last Rosh Hashanah in Meron davening at the *kever* of Rabbi Shimon bar Yochai with some of her children. She was very sick, and on the second day of Rosh Hashanah she collapsed. She was rushed to the hospital in Tzfas and was given four pints of blood. Her life was saved, at least for a short while. Her children believe that she got a few more precious weeks of life in the merit of Rabbi Shimon.

The last Yom Kippur

By Yom Kippur Henny was home and it was pretty clear that her end was near. Henny instructed her daughter how she wanted her children to pray for her on Yom Kippur. She told them again and again as Yom Kippur approached, "Don't daven for me. Because if I live or die, what's that going to change? Daven for the *geulah*. You only have a certain amount of time and energy. Daven for the *geulah*! If there's a *geulah*, I'll be fine anyway. Don't daven for me; daven for the *geulah*!"

The final *dvar Torah*

On Simchas Torah, too weak to walk, she was pushed to shul in a wheelchair where she could see her children and grandchildren dance with the Torah. After *hakafos* she returned home for the Yom Tov meal, where she gave her last *dvar Torah* to her many guests.

Henny shared with them a Torah thought from the Lubavitcher Rebbe. He asks: Why do we dance with the Torah closed and covered, rather than open? In order that all the Jews should feel equal dancing with the Torah. If we dance with it open some people would feel the Torah is only for smart people who understand it and know its deep meanings. Dancing with it closed sends the message that Torah belongs to all Jews.

The last dance

Perhaps one of the most bittersweet moments of Simchas Torah comes during the last dance of the men as they carry the Torah scrolls before returning them into the *aron kodesh*. It's joyful but sad. We happily sing the traditional songs *Se'u shearim rasheichem* and *l'shanah haba b'Yerushalayim*, but we feel sad too, knowing this is our last chance to dance with the Torah till next year. Goodbyes are sad.

This is the story of Henny's last dance with her family. It happened on Simchas Torah.

She had said her *dvar Torah* and the guests had left. Henny went to her room to lie down. Her children and grandchildren went with her to her room. Then her son-in-law Rabbi Avraham Willig came in and started singing. He looked at Henny's face, which was happy despite her pain, and said, "Ima, let's dance *hakafos* together." He took a scarf, and gave one end to Henny, while he held the other. Rabbi Willig danced back and forth, waving his end of the scarf in time to the singing, while Henny weakly waved her end from the bed. Soon all her children and grandchildren in the room were dancing in front of her. Henny smiled and waved her scarf. It was a moment of *simchah* for everyone there, but it was bittersweet, because everyone knew this was Henny's goodbye dance.

Henny knew she didn't have much time left. Too weak to inspire and impact on her family with words of Torah, Henny found an out-of-the-box way to get her final message across. She used music, and particularly one song that she asked her family to play over and over again during the last days of her life. The song expressed the thoughts she wanted to inspire her children with.

The last message, the final song

When someone knows they are about to leave this world they gain a different perspective on life, which is probably why the song she chose to be played again and again was "Just Like You." It's a song sung by a Jewish music group called "8th Day."

The song is based on the famous story of the Chafetz Chaim and a traveler who came from far away to visit him in his small, sparsely furnished home. The man was surprised that the house of the most famous and greatest rabbi of the generation was so bare. A wooden table and chairs; that was about it. No sofas, recliners, crystal chandeliers or breakfronts full of family silver.

The traveler asked the Chafetz Chaim why his house didn't have much in it.

The Chafetz Chaim answered: "Why are you carrying so little with you? Where is all your stuff?"

The tourist replied, "I'm just passing through."

Said the Chafetz Chaim, "I'm just like you, I'm just passing through."

These are the words of the refrain in the song that Henny loved, as her time on this earth slowly came to an end:

I'm just like you! I'm just passing through, just like you,
My heart wants to feel something that's real,
And my mind hopes to find treasures of another kind

And if you had my eyes you'd see...
A palace for you and me

Her daughter Elisheva felt that their mother wanted all her children to know that in this world —"we are all just passing through." The Chafetz Chaim — and, yes, Henny Machlis — realized that though this world is important, it's preparation for something immensely greater. We are in this world to make ourselves great through Torah and mitzvahs, which we bring to the next world, the one that's real and eternal — the world that really counts.

Final prayer

Throughout her life Henny had davened and said Tehillim. But at the end she didn't have the strength to do either. So she came up with a short prayer that she said over and over. "*Refuah sheleimah, Geulah sheleimah! Refuah sheleimah, Geulah sheleimah*!" They were her final prayers.

The end

Henny finally passed away on a Friday — the day of the week that had made her stay on earth so holy. Henny's *neshamah* returned to Hashem on the day of the week that she had dedicated herself to preparing food for all of Hashem's children, so they could all enjoy His holy Shabbos. It was *erev Shabbos,* the third day of the Hebrew month of Cheshvan, October 16, 2015.

A sad sign: The death notice announcing Henny's passing

Henny's legacy

Unlike others who leave behind wealth, jewelry and other possessions for their children, Henny had nothing like that to leave. What she left her children was best expressed by her daughter Sara.

"More than leaving us diamonds, my mother left us *tefillah* and *emunah*. She didn't leave me here alone. She left me with Hashem."

Interesting to note that there is a tradition among the chassidim of Ruzhin that whoever dies on the same date that the Ruzhiner Rebbe passed away goes straight to *Gan Eden*. His *yahrzeit* is on the 3rd day of Cheshvan — the date Henny passed away.

The last miracle

When the family got the terrible news of Henny's passing the first thing the family had to deal with was to have her buried before Shabbos. There wasn't much time to Shabbos and they didn't even have a grave for her yet! Rabbi Machlis went into high gear. The first step was to contact a cemetery to buy his beloved wife a burial plot.

His first choice was Yerushalayim's Har HaMenuchos cemetery. He contacted them but there were no graves available for in-ground burial. The other option was Har HaZeisim. But at that time it was unsafe because of the Arabs who lived nearby. Due to lack of proper security the Arabs often attacked Yidden visiting the cemetery. This was not a place to bury his wife!

There is another small cemetery in Jerusalem: the tiny cemetery of Sanhedria. It's in middle of a religious neighborhood, just a few blocks from where Henny lived in Maalot Dafna. *Tzaddikim* such as Rav Aryeh Levin, Rav Ben Tzion Abba Shaul, Rav Yehudah Tzadka and Rav Ovadia Yosef are buried there. However, because of its small size no graves have been available there for many years.

Rabbi Machlis simply could not find an appropriate place to bury his late wife. Meanwhile Shabbos was getting closer and closer. Rabbi Machlis was racking his brain. What to do? What to do?

In desperation Rav Machlis turned to a rabbi who was close to the Machlis family, and who was a member of the Council of the Chief Rabbinate. The rabbi immediately got to work and used his influence to persuade the *chevrah kaddisha*, the organization that deals with burials, to reopen its offices, which had already closed for Friday, to do a thorough computer search for an available *kever*.

Henny's tombstone

Searching through the data base they made an amazing, miraculous discovery! There was a grave available in the Sanhedria cemetery that no one had ever noticed! It had been bought years before by an American, but he had already died and was buried in America. He never used the plot he had bought in Eretz Yisrael!

It was clear to everyone that Hashem had arranged for Henny to be buried in a cemetery that contained the graves of so many of Yerushalayim's holy *tzaddikim*. It would be there, with all the other *tzaddikim*, that the righteous Henny Machlis would have her eternal resting place. It was where she belonged.

Though the funeral was late afternoon on Friday, hundreds came to weep over the great loss.

From the funeral the family immediately rushed to the nearby city of Beit Shemesh where they would spend Shabbos celebrating the bar mitzvah of one of Henny's grandchildren.

Darkness

In Yerushalayim as Shabbos began, the famous Maalot Dafna apartment, which had been filled with the sounds and spiritual light of hundreds of Jews of all types coming together to celebrate Shabbos together, was dark and quiet. Henny's light had gone to another world.

Shivah

Henny's memory was honored by thousands of people who came to comfort Rabbi Machlis and his children. Some even flew in from overseas just to visit the mourners. Great *tzaddikim* and *roshei yeshivah* took time from their busy schedules to come as well.

At the *shivah*. The family sat outdoors, because, for once, there wasn't enough room in the house.

The well-known Kabbalist Rav Gamliel Rabinowitz came, and declared that Rebbetzin Machlis's death was a *kapparah*, an atonement for all of Am Yisrael. Rabbi Reuven Elbaz, one of the great leaders of Sefardic Jewry, was so saddened by Henny's death that at the *shivah* he began crying uncontrollably. Then he asked to be allowed into the kitchen, where he touched her pots. Tears streaming down his face he declared, "These are the holy pots in which the Rebbetzin prepared food for so many thousands of people."

Henny's "holy" pots

Hundreds of other people came and in different words said the same thing: "She loved me like a mother." And each and every one of them spoke the truth.

The *shivah* was over on the Thursday after Henny's *levayah*. But of course the feelings of grief and loss remained. Tears don't stop when the *shivah* does.

After *shivah*

And there were questions to be answered. Would Rabbi Machlis still make Shabbos for so many guests with his wife gone? Would he start right after the *shivah* or wait a while, till the family came to terms with their loss? Would the famed Machlis open door slam shut?

Even at the *shivah* many wondered and asked Rabbi Machlis what would happen next.

He answered, "I just lost my wife. It's hard for me to think. Can I tell you after the *shivah*?"

And indeed, the Machlis family decided to continue their Shabbos hospitality. There would be no "down time" because they knew that would have been what Henny would have wanted and what was right to do.

This is the story of what went on in the Machlis home the very first Shabbos in Henny's home— without Henny.

Shabbos without Henny

On Friday, the day after the *shivah*, Yehoshua Machlis shopped and cooked, which was what he had done for most Shabbosos during his mother's illness, when she could no longer take care of it. One of Henny's daughters posted on the front door handwritten signs, in Hebrew and English, with the times of the three Shabbos meals. At the bottom, in colored ink, she wrote a prayer: "May there be no distress, grief, or lament on this day of our rest."

The challenge of celebrating Shabbos *b'simchah*, in joy, after their terrible tragedy was enormous. But the family rose to the challenge with faith and wisdom.

Surrounded by many guests and family, Rabbi Machlis began the meal by saying that Shabbos is an island of peace and joy. Everyone was invited to speak, but no one should mention anything that would cause sorrow or grief. He said, "We have to stay on the island of Shabbos."

The meal went on as it had for decades, good food, *divrei Torah* and Shabbos *zemiros*. At one point, though, a man who'd come late and who hadn't heard what Rabbi Machlis said started to talk about Henny and to cry.

Sadness on the island of Shabbos? Impossible! Immediately someone began singing the famous song, "*Mitzvah gedolah lihiyos b'simchah tamid* — it is a great mitzvah to always be happy." The moment of tears passed, and the men began to dance, trampling sadness under their feet, knowing that Henny would have approved and that she would be smiling.

Someone asked Rebbetzin Rena Tarshish, a well-known Yerushalayim educator, a question that bothered many who heard about Henny's death at the young age of 57, a question that may be bothering some of you who are reading this as well: How could this happen?

The question

Rebbetzin Tarshish answered with a story of the Chafetz Chaim

The Chafetz Chaim had a son-in-law who died young. His wife, the

Henny and Mordechai and the whole Machlis family at Yael and Yitzchak Zev's wedding.

Chafetz Chaim's daughter, asked her father, "There are so many people in the world. Why did Hashem have to take my husband?"

He gently answered, "It was your husband or a quarter of the world."

Sometimes one life saves millions. Sometimes we have no answers for what the Almighty does, because we are only human.

But Henny? Henny had no questions.

Words about Henny, and words by Henny

Henny taught in several seminaries, including one called Azamra. In their yearbook of 2011, there is a short tribute to each teacher. The entry for Rebbetzin Henny Machlis reads:

Through being a live example, you proved to us what life is really all about. We got to see first-hand how true emunah brings a person to true happiness and to all yeshuos in the world. We will never forget your warmth to every person and genuine ahavas Yisrael. Your great passion when saying a "Shehakol" will forever echo in our minds.

In the same yearbook Henny's message to her students was:

... So, my dear girls, remember to love yourself—to know there was never anyone like you and there never will be. You have unique talents, personality, wisdom, character traits, looks, abilities that HaKadosh Baruch Hu wants you to use, to shine your specific light in this world.

Remember, Hashem loves you like His only child—and everything you are and you experience is only to draw you closer to Him. Remember to speak to Him always. Remember not only to do what you can, but more than you can, because one more chesed will bring the geulah, and remember, I love you all too!

Those were Henny's words to her beloved students. And no doubt would be her words to all of us as well.

CHAPTER 16

Henny Is Still Helping People!

It says in the Gemara that *tzaddikim*, even after they die, it's as if they are alive. This doesn't mean that we can talk face-to-face with those great people, and that they are still with us here on earth (even though we wish they were!). It means that through the things they taught, the books they wrote, the students that follow them, *tzaddikim* are still influencing and helping us.

That's certainly true of Henny Machlis.

Sara Yoheved Rigler is a very talented writer. She was also a close friend of Henny's. So when Henny passed away, Sara Yoheved decided to write a book about her. It took her close to a year to write. She traveled to many places and spoke with more than 90 people who had known Henny.

Emunah with Love and Chicken Soup

Her book, called ***Emunah with Love and Chicken Soup***, is very popular. Almost 25,000 copies have been sold! People who knew Henny Machlis, and also those who didn't, were very inspired by reading about

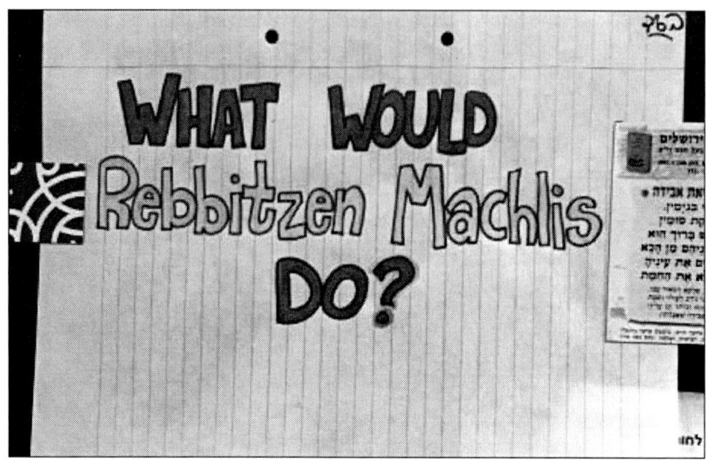

A reader put this reminder on her refrigerator!

her *emunah* and *chesed*. Many people from all over the world have told Mrs. Rigler that because of that book, when they have a problem the first thing they think is: **What would Henny do?** Some people even call them **WWHD Moments.** (That stands for: "What would Henny do?")

Here are some WWHD Moments that people have shared:

When there's love there's room — even in a taxi

A woman wrote to the Machlis family that reading about Henny's life had changed her. She shared a story of how thinking about Henny helped her do something nice. Once, she and a few friends were at a wedding together. They called a taxi to go home, but it was a snowy night and there was a long wait for a cab.

While they were waiting, a girl came over and asked if she could join them in their taxi. Even though there were too many people to fit in a taxi, this woman immediately said yes. She realized that it was because she knew that Henny would never have said no to someone on such a cold and wintry night. Henny would have *emunah* that it would all work out.

And, yes, it did! Instead of a regular taxi the company sent a minivan, and there was room for everyone!

A well-known rebbetzin told this story: She was on a plane, flying to a vacation spot. She took out her siddur to say *Tefillas HaDerech* (the prayer said when traveling). An elderly man sitting next to her looked over her shoulder and saw the Hebrew letters. "Can you really read that gibberish?" he asked. (The definition of "gibberish," for those of you who never heard the word, is "Words that mean nothing." A nasty thing to say about a Jewish book!)

The grumpy man on the plane

The rebbetzin didn't get insulted. Instead of answering him, she just smiled and said a few pleasant words to him. She soon realized that this man had once been religious, but had somehow stopped following the Torah.

A little while later, she started to read the book about Henny Machlis. The man peeked over her shoulder and started to read it as well. He even put on his special reading glasses!

At first the rebbetzin was a bit upset. I mean, it's weird, having some total stranger look over your shoulder at your book. But then she realized that it would be very good for him to read about Henny.

And read he did! He read over her shoulder for more than an hour, and then they started to talk about Henny, and how great she was, and how she'd become such a fine person. The man was now friendly and interested. Before they left the plane, he thanked the rebbetzin. "I found this book to be inspiring, and I really need to be inspired," he said. He wrote down the name of the book and told the rebbetzin he was going to buy a copy.

It would be nice to finish this story by saying the man did *teshuvah* and is now completely religious, but we don't know that. What we do know is that, once again, Henny Machlis had touched the heart of a Jew.

On the second *yahrzeit* (anniversary of the day of death) of Henny Machlis, more than 1100 women sat in a hall in Yerushalayim, listening to inspiring speeches given in her memory. One of the people speaking was Sara Yoheved Rigler, who'd written the book about Henny.

Henny makes a shidduch – after her passing!

She told a story about how Henny had made a shidduch — after she'd already passed away!

A woman had shared her story with Mrs. Rigler. Someone had suggested a shidduch for this woman's daughter. The boy was a wonderful young man, everything that the woman's daughter was looking for. Except for one thing: A few years before, when he was younger, he'd been pretty wild. But, the shadchan told her, that behavior was all behind him, he was a great person now.

The woman thought it over carefully, and then she called the shadchan back. The part about his past worried her. "I'm sure he's a fine boy," she said, "but he's really not for our daughter."

Later that very same day, this woman got very angry over something. Not wanting to lose her temper, she went to her room to calm down. While there, she picked up ***Emunah with Love and Chicken Soup***, Henny's biography. She opened it to a random page, and read how Henny said that if someone had changed, we should never hold their past against them.

Wow! It was like a message straight from Henny Machlis to this lady. She thought and thought, and finally picked up the phone to call the shadchan. "I've reconsidered. I'd like my daughter to meet this boy."

While Mrs. Rigler was still speaking, a woman in the audience stood up.

"I just want to say I know that story is absolutely true," she announced. "Because I am that mother. And my daughter is engaged to that boy!"

To mark a year after Henny's passing, the Machlis family had a *sofer* write a Sefer Torah in her honor. Usually, after a Sefer Torah is written, it is given to a shul to be used. In this case, the Machlises chose a very appropriate place for the Torah. It was brought to the Kosel, the Holy Wall that Henny loved, located near the place where the Beis HaMikdash had been built — and where the third Beis HaMikdash that Henny longed for so much will one day stand.

Henny's Sefer Torah

The Sefer Torah was brought there on her first *yahrzeit*. When

Happy crowds welcome the Sefer Torah to its new home

A circle of love and joy: Rabbi Machlis, center, holding the new Sefer Torah

The names of the Machlis "regulars" who are no longer alive, embroidered on the Torah cover

a Sefer Torah is brought to its new home, it's very much like a wedding: It is carried under a chuppah, with music and dancing. Though everyone missed Henny very much, there was great happiness too. They knew that Henny would be so happy to know that "her" Sefer Torah was now at the Kosel!

The Torah is covered with a beautiful velvet cloth. Henny's name is embroidered on the front. On the back, the family embroidered names of some of the people who often came to them, who have no children of their own to remember them. How happy Henny must have been to still be helping others!

Rabbi Machlis davens at the Kosel every Shabbos, and his minyan uses this Sefer Torah. At other times, although there are many hundreds of Sifrei Torah at the Kosel, people wait so that they can use this very special Sefer Torah.

CHAPTER 17

"Savta"

We've almost reached the end of our "Henny Machlis Journey." We've seen how a woman from a home and a background not so very different from our own reached very high levels of *emunah* and *bitachon*. We've read about *chesed* and Shabbos and davening and caring for each other and for Hashem. We've laughed a lot, we've cried a little, and we've learned to like — and love — Rebbetzin Henny Machlis, as a teacher, a parent, a friend.

Henny loved all her grandchildren very much. Here, she's holding baby Miriam.

Before we say goodbye, let's hear what some of the people who knew her best have to say about this amazing woman. We spoke with five of her grandchildren: Ushi, age 12, who lives in Yerushalayim; Nechama, age 13, from Ramat Beit Shemesh; Avigayil, also 13, who lives in Betar; Yosef, 15, who also lives in Betar, and Elisha, age 17, from Ramat Beit Shemesh.

Here — in their own words — is what they had to say about their beloved "Savta."

Henny's granddaughters Batsheva and Avigayil, their mother (Henny's daughter) Leah, and Henny's granddaughter who was named for her, Henna Rashe.

❖ *What are some of your special memories of your Savta?*

Nechama:

My grandmother, even though she spread love to every single Jew, had a warm, special place for a grandchild. It's not like she loved everybody else and we were dumped. She taught near our house every week, and after teaching she would give us money to buy ices for each kid. Even though she needed to get home she made it her business to chill with us a little; she always had the time for us.

Henny's granddaughter, Nechama

Every single kid had their own relationship with her. She was busy with so many people, so many situations, but she found the time and energy for each child and grandchild. She was there for everybody.

Elisha:

I'm her second to oldest grandson. I remember her Tehillim, that she would say. She would sit for four or five hours straight, saying Tehillim. I'm like, "Hi, Savta." She would wave to me, wouldn't say hi, just show me she was saying Tehillim. She had this huge Tehillim, huge letters. After a few hours she would get up, give me a huge, fat hug.

Henny's grandson, Elisha

The night before I had a test (entrance exam) for *yeshivah ketanah* (high school), I called her up, "Savta, daven for me." Next day, she called. "How was the test?" "Did you daven for me?" "Yes, I finished the whole Sefer Tehillim."

Avigayil:

I remember that she wouldn't go to sleep before she would daven Maariv. She would fall asleep and then wake herself up to daven.

Henny's granddaughter, Avigayil

Yosef:

First of all, I remember my grandmother waking me up for *neitz* (Shacharis prayers davened at sunrise) whenever I slept over at her house. She took me to the Kotel to daven *neitz,* and since then I love davening at *netz*. After that she would take me to Rav Usher's *kever*. Many times she would take me afterward to Kever Shmuel HaNavi. She would go to her usual bench and she would tell me that she needs to speak for a few minutes to Hashem. And she would start speaking, davening, screaming. Sometimes I would say, "Savta, I'm so tired," but she didn't hear me because she was so deeply involved in her davening.... Until I understood that I also need to speak to Hashem. Afterward she would buy me an ice cream, and then she would take me home.

Henny's grandson, Yosef

Ushi:

She used to daven with a big smile. She would take me and my brother to Kever Shmuel HaNavi and she would say, "Tatte, take care of everyone." And if she was on her way to an appointment and she was late, she would say, "Hashem, I'm late, help me." We had a school next to my grandparents' house, a *chiloni* (secular) school, and she used to go ask who wants candles for Shabbos.

Henny's grandson, Ushi

She really, really liked the Besht (the Baal Shem Tov); she would tell stories about him. I would call her and say, "I can't fall asleep." She would tell me stories for hours and then my mother would take the phone and say to her, "You can stop, he's asleep."

❖ *Were you ever in your grandparents' house for Shabbos?*

Nechama:

Of course. A lot of times. I was used to it, so it wasn't as "whoa!" to me, but it was outstanding.

My grandparents come through the door at the beginning of the meal to greet every person and say hi to everyone, ask their name. My grandfather shakes hand with the guys, and Savta would talk to the women and I would stand near her. She would bless them and tell them stories.

Sometimes I was creeped out. There were some strange people there. Savta would say: "You never know what the person is going through. We don't know who they are. Hashem brought them here for a reason. We will do our *hishtadlus*. They can look strange, you never know who the person is inside. Our *tafkid* is to do what we can and try to be nice to them." That blew me away!

Only after she passed away I realized how not ordinary she was. I was used to it. People talked about my Savta, but only now it's slowly coming to me that she was out of this world.

Elisha:

We'd come an hour before Shabbos and they're just starting to cook. The whole floor covered with groceries. A happening place.

Avigayil:

Shabbos was like a lot of people, 80, whatever; 100 people. She would serve. Now, after she died, I help in the kitchen. Me and my cousin go shopping for Shabbos and I serve. I'm there for many Shabboses, and when I'm there I serve.

I get a lot of comments: Why are you buying so much, what are you doing, who sent two little kids to shop? And I'm, like, whatever. I just say: I'm buying, I'm not playing, we have *hachnassas orchim*.

Yosef:

Her cooking wasn't the cooking of a regular person, her cooking was based on *tefillos*. Every time I would go for Shabbos she would make me special challahs, just for me, with the toppings I liked the most.

If I would get wild, even if I made a big mess in her house, she would call me on the side and speak to me so nicely, and ask me calmly, "Why are you making a mess? Please stop." She never screamed or got upset. After her talk with me she would give me a treat.

It was so much fun going to her house!

❖ *How did she make you feel special?*

Avigayil:

It's a hard question. In everything.

Ushi:

She had for each grandchild time, like she didn't have 14 kids. I had a problem reading, I would cry, kids make fun of me. She would say, "I'll help you." She'd say, "Ushi, I have all the time in the world, calm down, it's okay."

❖ *When did you see your Savta last?*

Nechama

On Simchas Torah, *hakafos*, she couldn't talk but she insisted on going to *hakafos*, she insisted. The whole shul was dancing there. She could barely talk but was giving *berachos*.

Elisha:

It never came up to my head once that she was going to die. In the Machlis house every day there were *nissim*. I never dreamt it would happen. She lived with Hashem all day. On Simchas Torah we danced, she started crying.

The summer before she was *niftar* I was in America and went to visit her in Sackett Lake by my great-aunt. I was supposed to go to camp that day but I wanted to see her. For literally half an hour she was telling me how much she loves me, and how much our whole family is great. How it's important to daven, don't worry about me, everything will be okay. That was the last time I heard her talking.

Avigayil:

I was in her house on her last Yom Kippur and I spoke with her for two hours at night. The thing is, it was Yom Kippur and our teacher spoke to us about Yom Kippur, and really scared me. Yom Kippur came in and I was really scared. I started throwing up. Savta calmed me. "What do you think, that on Yom Kippur Hashem says, 'You're so bad, you did this.' He's just showing that even though you did it He loves you and He's giving you another chance." I was talking for two hours. She died Friday. I was there the Tuesday before, but she was sleeping and I was scared to go to her.

Ushi:

Wednesday night. Me and my father and a friend came. I had a "shaker," a musical instrument, and we played for her for hours. She was moving her hands, I can't explain it. When we wanted to leave, she somehow said, "I want more, I want more."

Yosef:

I saw my Savta the week before she died. I was on *bein hazemanim* and I chose to spend the whole week at her house. I didn't want to go on any trips, I just wanted to be near her.

❖ *If you would paint a picture of your Savta, what would it look like?*

Nechama:

Her smiling, her big smile. Busy. She wouldn't just sit, she was always just doing something, saying Tehillim, davening, cooking, talking on the phone. I never picture her on a couch. Laughing, talking, always good things, busy with *chesed*. I picture her happy, doing something.

Elisha:

Definitely smiling and laughing and very, very happy. That's who she was. She would ask us to bring music and guitars. She didn't have such an easy life but she wanted to dance and dance.

I saw when she was going through a hard time, she would take me into her room and start singing and dancing with me.

Yosef:

I would paint a picture of her standing in the forest, screaming to Hashem.

Ushi:

A big smile on her face. And by Kever Shmuel HaNavi with a siddur in her hand and closed eyes.

Avigayil:

With a big smile, hugging someone. Her bear hug.

Though the heroine of our story is no longer with us, that doesn't mean the story is over. YOU can make sure the story continues by being inspired by her life to do *chesed*, to have more *emunah*, and to try to always be happy.

CHAPTER 18

Machlis Kitchen Recipes for Shabbos Hachnassas Orchim

We hope you enjoyed Henny's "Recipes for Life." Here are some real food recipes, straight from Henny's kitchen. Henny, her family, and volunteers would prepare these foods for Shabbos every Friday. This section was written by Henny's daughter, who always helped her in the kitchen.

Even if you are not interested in cooking at all, read through the recipes and you'll find some very interesting ideas. The main one is:

"Savta" Henny with a granddaughter and a guest, making challah dough

Don't be shy or embarrassed to daven for anything and everything while cooking and baking, or any time.

Since you will probably not be cooking for a hundred or more people, if you do want to follow the recipes ask a grown-up to figure out the quantity of each ingredient you will need.

Chicken Soup

35-40 carrots
20 medium-size sweet potatoes
15 medium-size onions
10 zucchini (medium size)
1 head of celery (optional)
25 chicken necks
50 chicken wings
Garlic powder, salt, and pepper to taste

Peel and cut all the vegetables into cubes. Fill ⅓ of a 50-liter pot with water and put it on a high flame. Add all vegetables and chicken and fill the rest of the pot with water (pot should only be ⅘ full so that it won't overflow). Add garlic powder, salt, and pepper according to your taste. Cook on a high flame until it boils. Lower flame and let simmer for anywhere between three hours and fifteen hours. It doesn't matter how much time you have to let it cook, the main thing is that you should daven while you cook that the food should have the taste of *Gan Eden* and that everyone who eats the soup should love Hashem, love Torah, love mitzvos, do *teshuvah,* and have *emunah*. Only Hashem puts His taste in the food; not us...

Kneidlach (Matzah Balls)

18 eggs
1 ½ cups seltzer
1 ½ cups oil
1 ½ tbs. salt

1 ½ tsp. pepper

About 30 ounces matzah meal

Beat all the ingredients, except for the matzah meal, together. Slowly add the matzah meal, mixing with a fork until the mixture is smooth and not runny. Put into the fridge for 20-30 minutes. Form balls and add to boiling chicken soup or a 20-quart pot of boiling salted water. You can make the balls any size, but remember that they will grow bigger while cooking! Cook for 10 — 15 minutes, on a medium-size flame.

This recipe makes between 100 — 150 kneidlach, depending on their size.

Make sure to daven that the kneidlach come out fluffy, tasty, and have a great texture, and that they should taste delicious to everyone who tastes them. May everyone who eats them enjoy the beauty of Shabbos food and may they be healed from any physical, mental, or spiritual illness.

Sweet Chicken Sauce — **for 25 chickens (100 pieces) (without necks and wings)**

100 ounces of ketchup (usually 4 — 5 bottles, unless you can get the extra-large size)

5 pounds brown sugar

2 big handfuls of garlic powder

1 cup of red sweet wine or 1 cup of orange juice

¼ cup soy sauce (optional)

Mix all ingredients together and pour over chicken. Please note that you can add the wine, orange juice, and soy sauce or NOT. We decide what ingredients to put into the sauce based on what we have in the kitchen. Again, the main thing is to daven that the chicken should be delicious and cook a perfect amount and be very soft, not underbaked, not overbaked, not burned. And that everyone who eats it should taste the taste of the mann that came down from Heaven.

Pour the sauce over the chicken. You can add sliced onions on top of the chickens before you put on the sauce. Cover while cooking.

If you are making the chicken in a deep tray and you are layering them, make sure to put sauce between each layer of chicken.

Bake at 450° for about two hours.

Sweet Potato Kugel

12-15 large sweet potatoes
3 cups flour
3 cups white sugar
3 cups brown sugar
2 cups oil
12 eggs
2 tbs. vanilla extract

Peel and cook sweet potatoes in a pot until soft. Drain the water. Mix all the other ingredients in a large mixing bowl until smooth. Blend cooked sweet potatoes until there are no lumps and add to mixture. Mix well and put into four 9X13 baking pans. You can top with cinnamon or with a crunchy topping (corn flakes, nuts, brown sugar). Bake at 350 for 30-40 minutes.

Daven while making the kugel that we should be sweet to other people and especially to our family members... Pray that Hashem should put His taste in the kugel and Hashem should remove all bitterness from the world and replace it only with sweetness...

Machlis Chulent

25 sliced medium onions
Oil for frying
25 pounds of cholent meat
Black pepper, garlic powder, sweet paprika,
brown sugar, a touch of silan

40 potatoes, peeled and cut into quarters

6 pounds red beans

6 pounds white beans

9 pounds barley

In a 50-quart pot fry 25 sliced medium-size onions. Fry until brown. Add chulent meat. Mix together. Add seasoning.

Then add the potatoes, red beans, white beans, and water to cover all ingredients and cook on a high flame until it boils.

Then add the barley. Cover the pot and cook until Shabbos, when you put it on a hotplate or blech.

...And now comes the real chulent:

Daven to the Ribono shel Olam that He should put His taste in this cholent, because every week for many years we could put the same ingredients in the chulent and every single week it comes out different, according to the *tefillos* of the people cooking. Rebbetzin Henny used to say that when you peel and cut onions and cry, don't waste your tears!!!!! Think about Hashem's pain and daven for the *geulah sheleimah* and that the Beis HaMikdash should be built. Daven that all the people who are suffering should be healed and have their personal *geulah*. Daven that all those eating this holy cholent on Shabbos should feel deeply connected to all the previous generations of our mothers, grandmothers, great-grandmothers, and great-great- grandmothers who put their *neshamahs* in the "cholent" and "chamin" (chamim is a Sefardic cholent) that they were lovingly cooking, as they prepared for Shabbos!

1-Bowl Quick Vanilla Cake*

24 eggs

4 cups oil

4 cups seltzer

12 cups flour

* When making batter with this much flour, one has to take "challah" from it. If you are making this huge batter, have your parent ask a rabbi how to do it.

12 cups white sugar
16 tbs. vanilla sugar
4 tbs. baking powder
pinch of salt

Beat eggs, oil, and seltzer together. Add all dry ingredients and mix well until there are no lumps. Put into four 9X13 baking pans. Make sure to daven that everyone who eats the cake should feel Hashem's love, and that they should love Torah and mitzvos. That they should feel the sweetness of Shabbos. Bake for 30-40 minutes on 350°.

Variations:

You can top with cinnamon and sugar / chocolate chips / blueberries.
You can swirl in chocolate syrup and make it into marble cake.

DONT FORGET TO SAY WHILE COOKING AND BAKING ALL SHABBOS FOODS:

Lichvod Shabbos Kodesh – In honor of the holy Shabbos

A Message from the Machlis kitchen:

As you finish your cooking and baking for Shabbos, it's a perfect time to add a special *tefillah* – that *this* Shabbos should be the Shabbos *that* will be enjoyed and observed by all Jews worldwide. And then add, with real feeling: Shabbat Shalom to Am Yisrael, wherever they may be!

Glossary

All words are Hebrew unless indicated otherwise

ahavas Hashem — love of Hashem.

Aron Kodesh — Holy Ark; (in shul) ark where the Torah Scrolls are kept.

baal teshuvah (pl. *baalei teshuvah*) — one who repents; one who returns to Torah-true Judaism.

baruch Hashem — lit., *Blessed is G-d*; an expression of gratitude for Hashem's goodness.

bein hazemanim — time off between semesters in yeshivah; intersession.

beis din — a Rabbinical court.

Beis HaMikdash — the Holy Temple in Jerusalem.

berachah (pl. *berachos*) — a blessing recited before performing a mitzvah and before and after eating.

bitachon — lit., *trust*; trust in Hashem.

chametz — leavened foods prohibited to own or eat during the Passover Festival.

chasan — a bridegroom.

chavrusa (pl. *chavrusas*) — a study partner.

chesed — acts of kindness; lovingkindness; charitable giving.

chizuk — encouragement; strengthening.

daven — (Yiddish) to pray.

davening — (Yiddish) 1. praying. 2. prayers.

dayan — rabbinical court judge.

dvar Torah (pl. *divrei Torah*) — a lesson from the Torah; a Torah thought.

eishes chayil — an exemplary Jewish woman.

emes — truth; truthfulness.

emunah — faith; belief in G-d; faithfulness.

Erev Pesach — Passover eve; the day before Pesach.

frum — (Yiddish) religious; Torah observant.

ganav — a thief.

geulah — redemption.

geulah sheleimah — the Final Redemption.

hachnassas orchim — hospitality; hosting guests.

HaKadosh Baruch Hu — lit., *The Holy One* (i.e., Hashem), *Blessed Is He*.

hakafah (pl. *hakafos*) — the encircling of the *bimah* seven times on the Festival of Simchas Torah, while dancing with the Torah Scrolls.

halachah (pl. *halachos*) — lit., *law*; (u.c.) the body of Jewish Law; Torah law and practice.

Hashem — lit., *the Name*; a respectful way to refer to G-d.

Hashgachah pratis — Divine Providence.

hisbodedus — meditation and introspection; thinking about your life, G-d, and other matters when you are alone.

hishtadlus — one's own efforts; the required effort.

kavannah (pl. *kavannos*) — intention, esp. when reciting a prayer or performing a mitzvah.

kedushah — holiness; sanctity.

kever (pl. *kevarim*) — a grave.

kippah (pl. *kippot*) — a yarmulke; a skullcap.

kiruv — lit., *bringing near*; outreach to teach people about their Jewish heritage.

kittel — long white garment worn by men during the Yom Kippur prayer services and at the Passover Seder, and, in Ashkenazic tradition, by the groom during the wedding ceremony.

Kosel — (also *Kotel*) the Western Wall, the holiest place in the world for all Jews because it is the last remaining part of the wall that surrounded the *Beis HaMikdash*.

lashon hara — lit., *evil speech*; derogatory speech; slander; gossip.

Mashiach — Messiah.

mekabel — to accept.

middah (pl. *middos*) — a character trait; an attribute.

Minchah — the afternoon prayer service.

minyan (pl. *minyanim*) - quorum of ten men necessary for conducting a prayer service; the group for communal prayer service.

Mishkan — Tabernacle; the portable Temple used by the Jews during their sojourn in the Wilderness and in Eretz Yisrael prior to the building of the *Beis HaMikdash*.

mussar — ethical teachings geared toward self-improvement; reproof.

netz — sunrise; the earliest time permitted to recite the morning prayers.

niftar — (n) a person who passes away. (v.) passing away.

oneg Shabbos — lit., *joy of Sabbath*; a gathering to celebrate the Sabbath; something that enhances one's joy on the Sabbath.

oveid Hashem (pl. *ovdei Hashem*) — a servant of G-d.

payos — sideburns or side curls.

posek (pl. *poskim*) — a halachic authority who defines what the halachah should be in a particular situation.

posek hador — the supreme halachic authority of a generation.

refuah sheleimah — lit., *a full/complete recovery*; a blessing for a complete/speedy recovery extended to an ailing person.

Savta — Grandmother.

sefer (pl. *sefarim*) — a book, specifically a book on holy subjects or a learned topic.

Sefer Torah (pl. *Sifrei Torah*) — a Torah Scroll.

segulah — a spiritual remedy.

seudah — lit., *a meal*, esp. one served on the Sabbath or a Festival.

shalom bayis — peace and harmony in the home; marital harmony.

Shamayim — Heaven.

sheker — (n.) a falsehood; a lie. (adj.) false.

shemurah matzah — matzah made of wheat that has been carefully watched from the time of harvest to ensure that it does not become *chametz*.

sheva berachos — lit., *seven blessings;* 1. the seven blessings recited at a wedding. 2. festive meals, celebrated during the week after a wedding, at which the seven blessings are recited.

shidduch (pl. *shidduchim*) — 1. match, esp. a marriage match. 2. a proposed marriage match.

shiur (pl. *shiurim*) — 1. a lecture on a Torah subject. 2. the required amount (e.g., of eating forbidden food to be considered a punishable act). 3. halachic amount.

shivah — lit., *seven;* the seven-day mourning period immediately following the death of a close relative.

siddur (pl. *siddurim*) — a prayer book.

simchah (pl. *simchas*) — 1. happiness, joy; a joyous occasion. 2. a happy occasion; a celebration, esp. a celebration of a family milestone such as a wedding, bar mitzvah, or a birth.

sofer — a religious scribe; scribe who writes religious materials such as a Torah Scroll, a *mezuzah, tefillin,* etc.

tafkid — mission; spiritual purpose.

talmid chacham (pl. *talmidei chachamim*) — lit., *the student of a wise person;* a Torah scholar.

tefillah (pl. *tefillos*) — Jewish prayer.

Tehillim — 1. (u.c.) the Book of *Psalms.* 2. (l. c.) psalms.

teshuvah (pl. *teshuvos*) — 1. answer. 2. repentance. 3. rediscovery of Torah Judaism. 4. a response to a halachic query.

tzedakah — charity; a charitable action.

yahrtzeit — (Yiddish) the anniversary of a person's passing.

yarei Shamayim — those who fear (are in awe of) G-d; connotes reverence for G-d, an all-pervasive attitude of piety.

yeshivah ketanah — an elementary school.

Yom Tov — a Jewish Festival.

zemiros — songs, esp. those sung at Shabbos and festive meals.